ETSY FOR BEGINNERS

Book 1 of *The Ultimate Guide to Selling On Etsy* Series

by Noelle Ihli and Jeanne Allen

CONTENTS

CONTENTS

INTRODUCTION

You're reading Book 1 of our series, *The Ultimate Guide to Selling on Etsy*. This three-book series will guide you through everything you need to know to start, run, and grow a successful shop on Etsy.

Book 1, *Etsy for Beginners*, is all about coaching you through the fundamentals of creating, setting up, optimizing, and operating a successful Etsy shop. Whether you're brand new to Etsy or already have an Etsy shop (but aren't sure laid the proper groundwork), Book 1 is for you.

Wondering what the other books in the series cover? Glad you asked!

Book 2 covers marketing and advertising: Think of it as an instruction manual on how to take your solid foundation and grow your shop into something bigger. The second book in The Ultimate Guide to Selling on Etsy series tells you how to make your product more visible within Etsy and across the web, for higher sales volume and faster growth.

Book 3 is all about expansion, scaling, and speeding up growth. We cover everything from branching into your own website, pros and cons of filing as different types of tax entities, advanced keyword and marketing strategies, and other logistics of turning your hobby into a thriving business.

If you know you want all three books, we've also packaged them into one resource, entitled *The Ultimate Guide to Selling on Etsy*.

Now that we're oriented, let's dig in!

First of all, why did I write this book series?

The Ultimate Guide to Selling on Etsy series is the culmination of everything I've learned since opening my own Etsy shop in 2013. I was a young mom with two kids, and I opened my shop as a way to carve out something that was just mine. Something that I loved to do, even if I was tired after a long day of tricking my toddlers into liking vegetables.

I had no idea what I was doing at first. But little by little, I learned. I planned. I threw spaghetti at the wall. I failed (I'll tell you all about those failures and mistakes, so you can avoid them!) I connected with other shop owners and learned what I could from them. I pored over the forums on Etsy. I experimented.

I did more of what worked. I took what I could from the failures. I kept learning. And growing

. . . Until I was so busy, that I had a decision to make. I couldn't keep my full time job and my Etsy shop because I was getting home at 5, spending time with my kids, and then working until midnight. So I made the leap. I quit my job and became a full-time Etsy shop owner. And it was one of the best decisions I ever made.

Etsy is an incredible platform. There's so much potential there. And if you know what works, you can be successful. I know because I did it.

If you're like me, you're probably feeling overwhelmed. You might be wondering whether you have what it takes. Whether your product is good enough.

Even if you've seen some success, you may still think of your artwork or handmade goods as your "little hobby." And I want you to knock that off right now. I've found that the people who run Etsy shops are some of the most creative, tenacious people I know. And I have no doubt that you are one of them. You can do this. You DO have what it takes.

Whether you're young or old, have 15 minutes a day to devote to your craft or hours, whether you're tech savvy or not, you can do this. I'm here to help.

That's why Jeanne and I wrote this book (Remember when I told you I found what worked? Well, Jeanne's brilliance and insight into the SEO/keyword/algorithm aspect of Etsy has worked magic in my shop. I'm going to let her introduce herself in just a bit). Jeanne and I are going to help you get started—and succeed—on Etsy.

There's nothing that makes us happier than hearing feedback from a new Etsy seller along the lines of "I was feeling overwhelmed, and now I just feel excited. I think I can really do this."

We promise down-to-earth, accurate, easy-to-follow information. No "secrets." No "one weird trick." Just what actually works.

Crafters are, well, crafty. They're creative and scrappy and strong. Handmade doesn't mean cute (I mean, it can). Handmade just means that you know how to roll up your sleeves and turn something ordinary into something incredible.

And that's exactly what we're here to help you do as you begin your journey on Etsy.

We'll address all the fundamentals in this book—shop components, listings, keywords, graphics and design, pricing, etc. Each of these topics is VITAL to laying the foundation for a successful Etsy shop with lots of growth potential.

So whether you're completely new to Etsy or or simply aren't seeing a lot of success yet (or want to feel confident that you've mastered the essentials before moving on to next-level strategies for growing your Etsy shop), let's talk fundamentals and solid foundation work. We'll walk you through each critical element of your shop so you can feel confident (and so you can start seeing those sweet sales come in!)

~Noelle and Jeanne

A LITTLE ABOUT US

Before we dive into the meat of this book, we want to introduce ourselves. We hope the advice in this book feels like pointers from a good friend: tips and advice from someone who will give the good stuff to you straight. To that end, we want you to know a little about who we are as people.

Noelle

I've already told you part of my life story (the part that involves my success on Etsy), which is arguably the most important thing you need to know about me (since you're reading a book series I co-wrote called *The Ultimate Guide to Selling on Etsy*).

But again, the whole point of this book is getting the real scoop on Etsy from a real person. So in that spirit, here's a little more about me:

First of all, I'm a mom. A boy mom to Luke and Max, and a cat mom to Michelle. When I'm willing to wear pants (which is less often than I aspire to wearing them), I can be found in mom jeans.

My husband Nate is the best person I know. He's hilarious and sweet and has an adorably bald head.

The two things I love most (in addition to Etsy and the aforementioned children and husband) are murder and horses. (Separately, never together.) I'm the weird horse girl you knew in elementary school who never grew out of that phase. And I'm the person Netflix is targeting when they roll out a new serial killer documentary, which is also the reason I have a keyed lock on my bedroom door.

My degree is in Spanish translation, which I don't use but don't regret because it opens up an entire world of television to me. In addition to being a mom and Etsypreneur, I've worked "traditional" jobs in marketing, social media, writing, and editing. I don't regret them either, even though I've never looked back from my decision to pursue Etsy as my full-time job.

That's me. I'm an introvert, which means that if you ever see me on a coaching video or webinar, I am definitely sweating. But I learned a long time ago that regularly doing scary, worthwhile things is a smart way to live. So here I am.

Jeanne

Like Noelle, I'm also a mom—to Kaylee, Eileen, and Tober. (Yes, Tober. The short story is that I let Kaylee name her baby brother when she was five. I swear I would have stepped in if she'd added too many Xs or Zs, but luckily, she hadn't learned those letters yet). And my husband Bryan is, like Noelle's Nate, adorably bald and pretty dang awesome and supportive. Especially when I decided to veer off a more standard career in technical editing and jumped headfirst into the world of Etsy selling.

As for pets, our family's latest foray is to adopt two mini rex bunnies, Ginsburg and Rocky Balboa. Who knew bunnies could be such great pets or that they have such big personalities? Rocky is in the habit of picking fights with animals much bigger than himself (chickens, cats, raccoons), and I'm pretty sure Ginsburg has clinical anxiety (possibly because of Rocky. Sorry Ginzy…). I've fallen in love with them both, surprising myself, since I've never been a huge animal person.

I thrive on political podcasts, fantasy novels, and group exercise classes (I'm 100% unmotivated to move my body without someone telling me what to do). And I really, really love coffee.

My degree is in Editing and SEO, and I started out in technical editing after college. I've edited everything from textbooks to computer manuals to journal articles on aerospace engineering (a.k.a., rocket science) and earthquakes. Technical editing has its perks (it definitely pays well), but one thing it's not is very exciting (at least, not for me). Working with Noelle the last three and a half years in the Etsy shop has been so much more fun. The work we do pulls from all the technical training I've had and has given me opportunities to learn a lot of new things as well.

I love our Etsy shop, and I love Etsy as an ecommerce platform. We're here to help you feel the love (and success) on Etsy too!

CHAPTER 1

The Anatomy of a Good Etsy Shop

We're going to kick things off with an anatomy lesson. Don't worry, you're still reading the right book. But just like med students need to get familiar with the individual parts of a human body before diving into surgery or physical therapy, you need to get very familiar with the different parts of your Etsy shop. You need to know where the heart is, what keeps it healthy, what different parts need to work correctly, and what could go wrong.

Much like a human body, each Etsy shop is unique. But they're also quite similar when you peel back the branding.

Even if you've already set up your Etsy shop, it's important that you DO NOT SKIP this chapter. You'd be surprised how many Etsy sellers are unaware that they've missed opportunities and left shop components half-baked in their rush to get selling. So, let's start with the basics of setup and continue with the anatomy of a healthy shop.

Setup: It's Really, Really Easy

Getting started on Etsy is extremely simple and honestly not worth a step-by-step here. You've got this, because Etsy has done a fantastic job of guiding you through the setup process to get your shop up and running as quickly as possible. It's possible to get a shop up and running in about five minutes with their walkthrough wizard.

Basically, Etsy strives to make setup super user-friendly. You can open and even run your entire shop on a phone or go seamlessly back and forth between your phone and laptop. Etsy's seller app for mobile is called "Sell on Etsy," and you can download it and start your shop by clicking "Don't have a shop?" right below the sign-in in the app.

All you really need is a product to sell and a niche that product fits into (which includes a pool of customers who would be interested in your product). Of course, zeroing in on how customers are searching for your product (through keywords), and which keywords fit your product best isn't quite so simple. But we've got your back, and we'll get to all that in good time.

As for the nuts and bolts of your actual Etsy shop setup, you'll need to create a Shop Name, Shop Policies, a logo, an About Section, a profile photo, and of course product LISTINGS. All of these components are important. But listings are the true lifeblood of your shop (the heart, if you will.) And because of how Etsy is set up—as a giant online craft bazaar—some people will purchase your products directly from your listings without ever clicking through to your shop itself.

This leads a lot of new sellers to focus only on listings without circling back to really hone their other shop components. If, during setup, you need to put "real good earrings" in your shop's About Section and come back to it later because you aren't sure what to write yet, do that. But remember to come back and give each part of your shop the love it deserves. Each of the aspects of your Etsy shop matters to potential customers and contributes to the overall impression you'll make: sloppy and rushed, or streamlined and professional. Basically, your Etsy shop is the sum of its parts. And the work you spend to strengthen each aspect of your shop strengthens the image you project as a whole.

Anatomy 101 of Your Etsy Shop

The following is an overview (anatomy 101) of an Etsy shop. You'll want to return to this section at different points throughout your journey to hone your Shop Name, About Section, Tagline, etc., as your shop grows and evolves. But for now, here's what you need to know about each major part of your Etsy shop and why it matters:

3

Shop Name and Title/Tagline

Your Shop Name and Tagline are closely tied with marketing and branding. But don't stress. If you are interested, we'll cover all things marketing in Book 2. For now, suffice it to say that your Shop Name and Tagline make a big difference to the first impression you cultivate for customers and even for SEO/search engine optimization (not just on Etsy, but on Google!). Choose something creative, intuitive, and make sure your Shop Name is available as a URL in case you decide to also open a Pattern by Etsy site (do a "domain name search" to find out if your Shop Name is available as a web domain). Etsy allows you to change your name if you want, so if you've made a horrible mistake you aren't doomed.

Your Shop Name should reflect what you do. "Earthling Cards" or "Cathy's Cards" are much better names for an Etsy shop that sells greeting cards than, say, "Cathy Creates" or "Greetings Earthling" (even though it's clever and I'm proud I thought of it). You want someone who hears your Shop Name for the first time or glances at it on google (and decides whether to click or not) to immediately have a solid idea of what you make. This helps google sort you out, it helps your customers connect with and find you, and it makes for a great first impression.

This can be tricky. Good names (and their corresponding URLs) are often taken. Be creative, but don't be weird. Be as clear as you can. And don't use weird cutesy spellings if you can help it. "Kathy Kreates" isn't going to do you any favors in Etsy or beyond. Shop Names have to be somewhat short, no longer than 20 characters. Your name can't include spaces, just be aware that you need to use capitalization to separate words (e.g, CathysCards, InspireArtwork, FourthWaveApparel).

Your Shop Tagline (or title) is a short (55 characters or less) blurb that should share briefly what you do. Your customers will see it just beneath your Shop Name, and Google may also display it in search results next to the name of your shop. So be keyword conscious without stuffing things in that don't fit. If you make greeting cards, stencils, and name tags, say that. Don't be coy. Keep it simple, and focus your Tagline around at least one great long-tail keyword (a phrase of two or more words) you can find.

For example, "handmade silver necklaces" is SO much more specific and useful than "necklaces." You're trying to imagine what your buyer would type into Google or Etsy that you provide. This can take some trial and error. Make it sound natural, do your best to think what ONE long-tail keyword phrase your customer would search to find your shop, and model your Tagline around that phrase or a series of phrases. A great example is "Small-batch jewelry: Handmade silver and quartz necklaces."

If you're too broad, you'll be easily forgettable and lost in a sea of competitors. It's a big ocean of shops and keywords out there. You want to hone in on what YOU have to offer. And you want to speak directly to those customers who are trying to find you. It's like your mating call (ew).

About Section

If a customer clicks through into your shop, the About Section is often the first place your buyers will click to see what kind of vibe you project into the Etsyverse. After all, Etsy is a handmade marketplace. It only makes sense that people want to know a little bit about the hands that made their product!

Your About Section tells who you are, where you came from. It humanizes you and connects you with your potential buyer (not to mention media outlets or social media collabs).

Aside from a good header image and a carefully curated first page of listings, your About Section is about as important as it gets to how customers will perceive you and your products. Here are the components of a really good About Section:

1. **Share your origin story.** It doesn't have to be epic. It just needs to be heartfelt, human, and explain in a satisfying way to your customers why you sell custom pickle dishes or felt hats or whatever you sell. Did your mom teach you to sew when you were younger and that was when you realized you were born to do creative things? Did you craft a pickle dish at a ceramics workshop and become the talk of the neighborhood after a backyard barbecue? SHARE THOSE THINGS. Humanize yourself. Endear yourself. Do you have family or employees involved in what you make? Make them part of the story too.

2. **Set yourself apart.** A lot of people make similar stuff on Etsy. Before you dive into your About Section, take a few minutes to write down the top three things that set you apart from the crowd. Do you use a special kind of ink? Are you a person of color in a white-dominated industry? Do you paint with your toes? Lead with this information proudly instead of burying it at the end of your About Section. What makes you unique makes you human and connects you to potential buyers.

3. **Use all five photos.** You have the option to include up to five high-res photos in your About Section. USE THEM. Each one is worth 1,000 words (at least). Etsy is about buying from a human, remember? And what medium best tells the story of a human, relatable shop owner? Photos. Use natural lighting and a variety of compelling, interesting photos that show yourself, your shop members, and any aspects of how you make or create your products. Think of it as a "behind the scenes" photoshoot that shows who you are visually. If it makes sense, include kids, animals, family members, and pets (everyone loves these things). Avoid straight-to-camera shots in all of the photos. You want this to feel like a glimpse into your world.

4. **Make a shop video.** This one is daunting for most people. But armed with a smartphone and free video editing software (OpenShot is a great option), you too can have a shop video. Keep it simple. Show footage of your studio, your workspace, your employees, your product. Again, probably don't shoot stuff straight-to-camera or you'll look like a used car salesman. Make this a "behind the scenes" glimpse, as if your potential buyer just opened up a little portal to your shop. Pair it with neutral, positive music (but nothing copyrighted—you can find free tracks in a variety of places like the Free Music Archive or Jamendo.com).

5. **Include photos of each shop member.** In addition to your About Section's five photos, you can upload a photo and an "about" description for each person in your shop (including yourself). Keep these descriptions concise, upbeat, warm, and relatable. Not everything you share has to be about your business, but at least some of it should be. You've already told everyone why you started your shop: Focus this blurb for each shop member on personal details. Do you have five kids and an obsession with hot hula dancing? Do you have a raccoon for a pet who sometimes accompanies you to the studio? Share these details.

Remember, keep everything as professional, tight, and human as possible. Ask several trusted friends to look at your photos and read your About Section copy (text) and offer critiques (use that word, you're not asking for a pat on the back). If you can't find someone to do this, join a seller's forum on Etsy and offer to exchange feedback. This is well worth your time.

Don't have the money for professional photos for your About Section? No problem. Student photographers often offer discounted rates. You can also do a lot with your smartphone, a little patience, and a willingness to learn some tips on lighting and composition (check out Chapter 3).

Shop Sections

Shop sections are like the skeleton of your shop. They help keep your shop navigable and organized for both you and your potential customers. You're allowed to have up to 20 shop sections, which will appear on the left side of your shop. These sections help organize your shop into categories that either help or confuse the crap out of your customers.

Do some serious thinking about how you want to organize your products. Is it by color? That might make sense if all of your earrings are quite similar and differ mostly by color. Is it by theme (e.g., ocean paintings in one category, and forest paintings in another)? Decide on the factor that's most important to your buyers that intersects with what sets your listings apart from each other, and divide things up that way.

Keep your section names simple and short (as with your Shop Name, you've got 20 characters to work with). Etsy will automatically create an "All Listings" section for you that you can't remove, as well as an "On Sale" section that shows what you've got on sale. The rest is up to you.

Listings can only be added to ONE section (unless they're on sale, in which case they'll appear in the On Sale section and whatever other section you've assigned them to).

TIP: If at any point you decide you hate your shop sections or want to shift things around, that's easy to do en masse from your listings manager. Within the Listings section of your Shop Manager, you can select (check the box in the bottom left corner of a listing) as many listings as you like, click "Edit Options," and swap them into a new shop section in one fell swoop.

TIP: Once in a while, I forget to assign a listing to a shop section when it's created (this isn't mandatory. You can have listings with no shop section). These listings will appear in searches, and in your "All Listings" section, but nowhere else. This is a bummer for visibility. Don't do this.

TIP: Keep it simple, try to make things intuitive for your buyer, and use sections to keep your shop organized and navigable. This makes you look smart, savvy, and on-top-of-things to buyers.

Shop Announcement

Your Shop Announcement appears prominently right below your Shop Name and logo. You can change this as often as you like. And you can add quite a lot of text (but you probably shouldn't. Only the first two sentences or so show automatically without the buyer having to click "read more"). Keep this short, to the point, and personable. I choose to tell buyers that if they sign up for my newsletter, they'll receive a code for 15% off their order (we talk about why you want an email list and how to do this in Book 2). At other times, I've chosen to relay information about holiday shipping cutoff dates, a fun quote that appeals to my buyers, or a sale announcement. Use concise, tight copy ("copy" in this case and throughout the book simply means "writing"), and let your personality shine a little without being unprofessional.

Etsy will show your buyers how recently you updated this announcement, so make sure you tinker with it regularly to cultivate the impression of a doting shop owner who is heavily invested in their craft (because that's probably highly accurate, but it's easy to forget to update this section!).

Shop Updates

Shop Updates work as both free advertising and another tool to help you create a good impression on potential buyers. They get sent via notifications to anybody who has favorited your items, your shop, or made a purchase from you. Pretty cool, huh? These updates are sort of like Etsy's in-house social media tool. You have to make updates from your phone (it's hidden under the marketing tab on the Etsy

Seller's App), and ideally these posts are quite similar to your social media feed with updates, announcements about sales, and general frivolity and behind-the-scenes goodness.

Posting Shop Updates regularly shows that you are an engaged shop owner (and Etsy loves engaged sellers!). If you make one Shop Update in 2016 and never again, people may worry that you are dead or just a deadbeat. Post regularly to show that you are IN THIS. Sparse or nonexistent updates can make customers worry that you might not really be active in your shop—that you might not respond to questions promptly, ship items on time, or keep up with current trends. And that kernel of worry can quickly translate into clicking away from your shop (especially for larger or important purchases).

Your updates appear on your shop homepage, toward the bottom underneath your reviews. And your customers can peruse old shop updates to get an idea of what you've been up to over time. While you have the option to cross-post shop updates to other social media platforms like Instagram, I wouldn't recommend it. Cross-posting too much too often teaches your audience to ignore you on most of your channels, since you post the same stuff there anyway.

TIP: Shop updates are clickable! And you can link products to each shop update. Aka, if you have a brand new purse and you share the news with your fans, they can click the shop update to be taken directly to the purse's listing. Amazing, amirite?

TIP: Don't use photos that are already part of your listing images. Show your product being made, behind the scenes, interacting with a customer, a sale or coupon announcement, or "coming soon" teasers about stuff you have in the works so your customers know to stay tuned.

Shop Banner, Shop Icon, and Profile Photo

Your **shop banner, shop icon, and profile photo** combine to create the face of your shop.

Your shop banner is the big banner image that covers the length of your Etsy shop homepage at the very top. In the past, Etsy used a more narrow banner—which you still have the option to use, but I wouldn't recommend it because it doesn't show up on mobile.

This shop banner should set the tone for your shop visually, since it's one of the first things a buyer sees when exploring your shop. Keep it simple, make it beautiful, and include some of your favorite products. You can create a basic collage of cohesive photos of your products (Canva is a great way to do this easily). Or you can show one fantastic "lifestyle" image of people using your product (we'll talk about photography in more detail in Chapter 3). Whatever you do, make it beautiful, impactful, and keep it simple. Don't try to cram in a lot of text. In fact, I prefer not to use any text because your buyer's eye will move right along to your shop icon.

I'm not going to give you the exact dimensions of your shop banner, because Etsy keeps changing this and they will inevitably make a change as soon as I publish this, which will leave you feeling confused and distrustful. SO. Do this. Google "Etsy shop banner dimensions." It will take you three seconds or less. Make your shop banner this size, and make it a 75-dpi JPEG (for some reason, Etsy freaks out about pngs a lot of the time).

If you're stumped as far as what you want your shop banner to look like, browse through other Etsy shops that catch your eye and you'll start to get an idea of what looks nice to you. Do this until you get a sense of what you're after. Don't snag anybody's idea wholesale, but inspiration is always kosher.

Your **shop icon** is a small image that appears underneath your shop banner, to the left. This should, in most cases, be your logo (and yes you DO need a logo, even if you're a newbie. You can create one for free or very inexpensively, something we talk about extensively in Book 2). Your Shop Name will appear right underneath your logo, and visually it just makes sense. Having a logo as your shop icon projects legitimacy, professionalism, and the idea that you are highly invested in creating your products and running a top-notch shop. Make sure you have one.

Your **profile photo** (or shop owner photo) appears beneath your shop banner on the right. This should be a close-up of you (don't make your buyer squint, this photo is already pretty tiny).

Your shop banner, shop icon, and profile photo should look COHESIVE. Don't include an edgy, avant-garde banner with a cutesy logo and a serious black and white photo of yourself. You want your buyer to say "Ahh, all the pieces here fit together" instead of "What is going on, did three different people put this Etsy shop together?" (Maybe they did, but you don't want your buyer to think that.)

The result of a beautiful shop banner with a smart and cohesive logo, along with a photo of you, and the name of your shop (this will automatically populate from Etsy's info) is that your customer has a LOT of information at a glance about you. And a budding sense of trust that you know what you're doing.

Listings: The Heart of Your Etsy Shop

Congratulations! You're cruising through Etsy Anatomy 101. Drumroll, please. Because ladies and gentlepeople, we have reached the HEART of your Etsy shop: Your LISTINGS.

The truth is, the vast majority of Etsy users won't ever see inside of your shop. Which means that while the individual components of your Etsy shop (the ones we've just covered in Anatomy 101) are very important and can have a big impact on your growth and how potential customers view you, some components of your Etsy shop are more important than others. Think of your Shop Name, About Section, and Updates like your Etsy shop's mouth. Your shop can survive even if they aren't doing much talking (it's not ideal, but you get my point!). But you can't survive without your heart: listings.

Here's the thing: Most of the traffic to your Etsy listings will come from Etsy users who don't know you exist a full-blown shop (yet) and are scrolling through MANY different listings (often very quickly) that populate after they type a query into the Etsy search bar —until something catches their eye. Your goal is to make sure that it's YOUR listing that catches their eye.

Not to mix too many metaphors (actually that's one of my favorite things), but think of your individual listings as your shop's ambassadors. Each one is an opportunity to catch a buyer's eye and entice them to click into your shop or simply buy without ever knowing much about you.

Imagine the moment your buyer clicks on a listing, or clicks on your shop from an ad somewhere as a "first impression." Of course, in Etsy as in real life, first impressions will only get you so far (see the rest of the chapters in this book on customer service, listings, tags, and so forth!), but first dates can often mean the difference between a sale and a hard pass.

That first impression determines whether a buyer is interested in continuing the conversation by reading more of your listing description, adding stuff to their shopping cart, "favoriting" a listing for later, checking out your shop and other products, or making a purchase.

Basically, you want to turn your Etsy listings into the Brad Pitt of e-commerce shops—highly likely to make a good impression and spark interest and interaction. And happily, you are the god of your Etsy shop. You determine whether you end up with Brad Pitt or Brad from next door. Or Frankenstein's monster (don't worry, you won't end up with that. I've got you).

Creating listings that make a good first impression and entice buyers to click is the first big hurdle toward earning a customer (Chapter 2 is actually all about listings, so I won't delve into the details here). For now, what you should understand is that we have reached a VITAL organ when it comes to your Etsy shop. Listings are the lifeblood of your shop. And for that reason, they deserve the bulk of your attention and time.

Reviews

Reviews aren't quite heart-level anatomy. But they are pretty darn important. Like ... maybe the butt. Not always pretty, often overlooked, but HIGHLY important.

Your shop reviews show up under ALL of your displayed listings, within any given listing a customer clicks, as well as on your shop homepage. These reviews are often the VERY first thing a buyer will check (and may even be the reason they click (or don't click) on your listings. Across the board, surveys show that 97% of Etsy customers look at reviews before deciding whether to make a purchase. That's almost every single potential customer.

So reviews are arguably one of the most important parts of a healthy Etsy shop. They are highly visible in multiple locations, and they can either signal major confidence to potential customers—or major red flags. We'll talk more about reviews and customer service in Chapter 6, but reviews are such an important part of the first impression you create for buyers that we need to talk about them here, too.

You should aim for five stars whenever possible. A shop with many five-star reviews gives your buyer confidence that other people have been in their shoes (making a decision about whether to click "add to cart"!) and they don't have any regrets.

The importance of good reviews can't be overstated. The more the better. Do everything possible to ensure that the reviews you DO have are stellar. I know what you're thinking: Are reviews really something I can control? I can't do anything about it if a customer decides to go all Rambo on me and hit me with a 1-star. And you're a little bit right. But you actually have more control than you think. You CAN heavily influence whether or not people leave five-star reviews. And you can help avoid (and soften the blow) of the negative reviews. We'll get to all that in Chapter 6. For now, just remember: Reviews are IMPORTANT. Don't neglect them, even if you sort of want to.

Featured Listings

In our Magic School Bus journey through your Etsy shop anatomy, another very important part is your **featured listings.** And yes, these are just your listings, four of them. But these particular listings are extra important and have a prominent and visible place in your shop. They're kind of like beckoning hands that say, "If you like these, there's more inside!"

Featured listings appear right below your shop banner and icons. You get to pick four listings you love the very most and that you feel will speak to your potential buyers. Anyone who clicks on a link to your shop will see these listings first.

Switch up your featured listings depending on holidays and what seems to be selling well. Etsy shows buyers whether or not a listing is a "bestseller" or "in 25 people's carts" or "on sale!" Stack some if not all of these hot-sellers in your featured listing bracket right up top. This acts as compelling social proof for potential buyers. Basically, "Whoa, look at how many other people love this! I love it a little more too now."

It can be a little confusing to swap and update featured listings. At the bottom of your Shop Manager, you'll see your Etsy shop listed under "Sales Channels" (see image below). Click the "pen" icon next to your Shop Name and you'll be taken to an editable version of your shop as your customers see it. You'll see your Featured Items section with another pen icon in the bottom right corner. If you click that and then "edit queue," you'll be able to choose which four listings you want to feature and see how they look to customers.

TIP: Try to show a good variety in your featured listings (price point, type of product, color variety, etc.). Customers often eyeball these as a way to gage what else they might find in your shop.

TIP: If you're pushing a sale item or something important on social media, feature it as a featured listing as well. This helps your buyers make an immediate connection with the product upon visiting your shop.

Things I learned the hard way: I'm guilty of forgetting to make key changes to my featured listings during busy seasons. At one point I looked at my shop in February and realized I'd forgotten to swap out my Christmas seasonal featured listings. That looked SUPER professional to buyers (eye-roll).

First-Page Listings

Moving right along from Featured Listings, of major importance are your first-page listings (there are 36 per page). These listings create a strong visual story of your Etsy shop as a whole and are going to be the most-seen listings (right after your featured listings) in your shop.

You should know that you have the option in Etsy to arrange your listings in a custom order or "newest first." You can rearrange listings by clicking the pen icon next to your Etsy shop at the bottom of your Shop Manager (under "Sales Channels") and selecting "Rearrange Items" (top right of "All Items"). Most of the time I'd strongly recommend choosing a custom order. It gives you significantly more control over the impression you create for your buyers. Unfortunately, any time you create a new listing for a product, it's going to appear at the top of your page until you move it around in editing mode. Make sure to edit your first-page listings regularly, since best-selling listings change throughout the year and holiday seasons, and any time you add a new listing it'll change the look of your first page (since it appears at the top).

Since I don't create brand new listings that often (maybe twice per month), I like to maintain a lot of control over how my first-page listings look. Like my featured listings, I try to show a good mix of products in different price tiers, styles, and colors. I want this first page to be as visually interesting as possible and encourage my customers to click one or more of those listings and see my shop as an oyster of possibilities. I also like to include a lot of my best-sellers and shirts that seem to be perpetually in "10 people's carts."

If not much appeals to a buyer on the very first page, they're not super likely to keep clicking through in hopes that you have good stuff buried in page 4. They're gonna click out of your shop and your life. Page 2 and 3 are of secondary and tertiary importance, because if an eager buyer loves what you show on page one, they'll likely keep clicking.

TIP: I don't worry that much about page 4 onward. Most people just DON'T click that far. Those listings WILL be seen when they come up in search for your buyers who type in relevant search queries, but it's only really essential to order pages 1-3.

The Knee Bone's Connected to the Leg Bone: Creating Synergy in Your Shop

Synergy is the phenomenon that happens when something becomes greater than the sum of its parts. And that's exactly what happens when you spend the time to create an Etsy shop in which each aspect of your shop's anatomy pulls its weight.

The more cohesively the different parts of your Etsy shop work together, reinforce each other, and complement each other, the more you'll appeal to your customers (and even earn repeat customers). You're aiming for tight listings that sell your brand as a whole (along with individual products), a Shop Name that strikes just the right balance of informative and creative, a visually appealing first impression with a cohesive shop banner and photos, and copy that reinforces the vibe and products you're peddling.

Here's a high-level overview of what you're trying to accomplish with that synergy:

- Your shop banner, listing images, and featured images are clear, beautiful, and cropped properly. **What buyers take away:** This person is a professional. What I see is what I get, and I anticipate a beautiful, interesting product.

- Your shop looks organized and professional (e.g., no spelling errors).**What buyers take away:** This person knows what they're doing. They're going to take care of me.

- Your shop sections are concise, descriptive, and intuitive. **What buyers take away**: It's fun and interesting to explore this shop—instead of confusing or annoying.

- Your "About Section" includes helpful, interesting information about your business origin, you as a person, and what you sell (instead of being sparse or blank). **What buyers take away:** You're a real person! I feel connected to your story and have a better understanding of why your product differs from something I could buy with two-day shipping on Amazon.

And that's your Etsy shop anatomy! Strut your stuff with confidence, you sexy animal. You're well on your way to becoming a self-actualized Etsy shop with a killer bod.

CHAPTER 2

All About Listings and Search Algorithms

Like we keep saying, good listings are your key to success as an Etsy seller. You may be selling the coolest, most unique product, an item that sells like hotcakes at an in-person event, but on Etsy your product is doing virtually nothing. The big difference is that in-person sales connect you and your customer directly while online sales take place through an intermediary, in this case, *Etsy's search algorithm.*

All this is to say that your listings need to deliver the right signals to Etsy's search algorithm. It's the gatekeeper between your product and your potential customers. If you don't know how to speak the algorithm's language, you'll have trouble selling even the best products.

How Etsy's Search Algorithm Works

So, how does Etsy's algorithm actually work? The basic process goes like this:

- Step 1: A potential customer types what they want into the search box, say "birthday gift for mom."

- Step 2: Etsy's algorithm pulls all the listings containing this search phrase and similar *keywords* and displays them in order based on *certain ranking factors* (which we'll discuss in more detail below).

- Step 3: Your customer sees your product, clicks on it, places it in their shopping cart, and buys it.

Like Google's search algorithm, the details of how Etsy's algorithm works are a closely guarded secret. However, Etsy has been pretty open in recent years about many of the factors they use to determine a listing's rank.

We've been around the block enough times (and experimented enough with different factors) to tell you with a high degree of confidence that the following factors are absolutely key to communicating with Etsy's algorithms. Now, some things are going to change over the years. The algorithm is going to get smarter. But these lynchpin factors aren't going away anytime soon. Because they're important to customers, and therefore they're important to Etsy's algorithm.

Fundamentals of a Listing That Speaks to Etsy's Algorithm

Remember at the beginning of this book when we told you that your Etsy shop is the "sum of its parts"? Well, here's why that's true from a search algorithm perspective. Etsy's algorithm gives each shop a score internally based on how professional and complete that shop is, the quality of its listings, and customer experience (largely shop reviews and shipping accuracy). We're going to refer to this score as your "shop quality score." You won't be able to find out exactly what this number is (that's the secret part), but it greatly influences the rank your listings get in search, and it's constantly changing based on how you and your customers interact with your shop. So it's pretty important.

When a buyer types a search query into Etsy, the algorithm first pulls all of the relevant listings—ones containing the customer's search phrase and similar keywords. And then the algorithm ranks these listings based on the shop quality scores. Even if you sell exactly what the customer is looking to buy, if your shop has a low quality score, your relevant listings will rank too low to be found.

Chapter 1 talked about how to optimize the various parts of your shop. This is the first step toward raising your shop quality score. The second step is creating consistently good listings. In this chapter, we'll be talking about the main factors that Etsy's algorithm cares about when it comes to listings—titles, tags, attributes, and descriptions—as well as ways to engage with your listings that send positive signals to Etsy's algorithm and are guaranteed to raise your shop's quality score.

High-Quality Images

Since it's text-based, Etsy's search algorithm doesn't directly interact with or evaluate your images, but it does take into account how often customers click on and engage with your listings, and these factors are often a direct result of having high-quality thumbnail images. (We'll talk about thumbnail images specifically in much more detail in Chapter 3.)

Here's what Etsy's search algorithm considers when it comes to images:

- You've used all 10 images. Using all 10 images seems to give you a tiny edge in rank, so if you can, use all the image slots available even if you fill the extra slots with images that don't directly relate to the listing (like pictures of you in your studio, promotional, or brand images).

- You've linked images to all of your variations (e.g., different colors and styles), and link each variation to the related image. This is a cool new feature that Etsy recently (in early 2020) added, and it's super handy for customers who want to see exactly what each variation looks like. It'll also give your listing a tiny boost in rank, but it's not something to stress about, especially if you have a lot of variations or your variations don't look much different visually.

- Use simple, clear, correctly sized images (we'll talk ALL about images in Chapter 3). Like I said before, while Etsy's algorithm won't be evaluating the actual QUALITY of your images (i.e., how appealing they actually are to a person), your customers will. And how often your customers click on your listings because they LOVE your images will send strong signals to Etsy's algorithm.

Properly Crafted Listing Titles

Listing titles are arguably one of the most important ways you communicate with Etsy's algorithm. Specifically, the first **keywords** you use in your listing title.

I want to take a slight diversion here to define some terms. There are two types of keywords I'll be talking about in this chapter. The first type is **short-tail keywords**: these are words or phrases that describe general categories of products, e.g., women's shirts, silver earrings, blankets. You can recognize a short-tail keyword on Etsy by how much competition it has—do a generic search for "women's shirts," and you'll see that over 5 million listings come up (Yikes!). Any keywords/phrases that bring up more than 50,000 listings are considered short-tail keywords (and saturated markets). Generally, you'll want to avoid most short-tail keywords in listing titles and tags.

Instead, try to use **Long-tail keywords**: these are more specific phrases that describe niche products, and they're much more effective at bringing in sales. Why, exactly? People typing long-tail keywords into Etsy's search box are usually the customers that know what they want. They have something specific in mind and are ready to buy it as soon as they find what they're looking for. It may feel counterintuitive to use long-tail keywords that attract a smaller crowd, but the truth is that more eyes on your listings doesn't necessarily translate to more sales, especially if the people seeing your listings are just there to browse rather than buy.

I'll also be mentioning **queries** throughout this chapter. Queries are the keywords or phrases customers on Etsy are typing into the search box—queries ask the algorithm, "Do you have any listings offering 'hand-stamped silver necklace charms'? Or 'dinosaur baby blankets'?" And the algorithm answers the query, "Why yes, here are 6,000 or 10,000 or 5 million results you might be interested in."

All right. Now that you understand the terms I'll be using in this chapter, let's get back to the topic at hand: Listing titles. A truncated form of your title appears under your thumbnail image in search results, and your full title appears next to your image after someone clicks your listing. In its official guidelines, Etsy encourages sellers to write titles for their customers (as opposed to trying to game the algorithms). After all, titles are the first text your prospective buyers will encounter when visiting your listing.

However, in reality, Etsy's search algorithm doesn't distinguish between a human-readable title and a long list of keywords separated by commas. In fact, Etsy actually rewards *keyword stuffing* in titles, which is why most sellers do just that. If you've spent any time studying Google SEO, you'll balk at this. Google doesn't reward keyword stuffing. But Etsy does. (Although Google seems to have accepted that Etsy sellers are going to stuff keywords in their titles and doesn't punish individual listings for this. Whew!)

Here's how to write listing titles the algorithm will understand:

General Good Practices

- Put your BEST keywords first. Don't bury the lede. The very first keyword you use in your listing title is given the most weight by Etsy's search algorithms. Try to put your very best keywords within the first 40 characters of your title.

- Use a mix of descriptive long-tail keyword phrases and short-tail, generic keywords. In those first 40 characters, focus most on finding really good long-tail keywords. For example, lead with "abstract acrylic pour painting on canvas" instead of simply "acrylic art" or "abstract painting." Place shorter, more generic keywords further down your title. This will help you connect with customers who want exactly what you're selling, a.k.a., the kind that actually buy stuff.

- Describe your item precisely and with as much detail as possible within the 140 character limit.

- Use as many keywords and keyword phrases as possible, and separate these with commas (again, keyword stuffing is perfectly acceptable in Etsy titles).

- Avoid whimsical product names, the name of your company (unless it's super well-known and associated closely with your product), and any other fluffy, non-descriptive phrases in the title. If you want to include any of these, place them as close to the end of the title as possible. (Better yet, put those fun, creative product names in your description and keep your title focused on keywords.)

- Once you find a good long-tail keyword, repeat it throughout your listing using different variations as many times as possible (But don't bother with plurals or misspellings, Etsy's algorithms view them the same way so you'll be wasting valuable title space). This is especially important for tags, which I'll discuss in a bit.

Tools for Picking the Best Keywords and Phrases to Use in Your Title

Finding the BEST keywords can feel like throwing darts in the dark. But you don't have to endlessly guess and hope you hit the target. The following tools will tell you exactly what customers are typing into the Etsy search box so you know exactly which keywords to use in your.

- Use the **Etsy search box** to type in keywords you'd use to describe your product and see if Etsy autofills phrases that describe it. This strategy will definitely give you ideas, and it *does* represent what customers are typing into the search box. However, keep in mind that Etsy's autofill phrases are taken from the most *recent* searches rather than the most popular. So if you use this method, you'll have to watch how your keywords are performing using Etsy Stats and adjust accordingly.

- **Mimic other sellers' titles**. Do some searches for your chosen keywords, and see if products similar to yours come up. Craft your title based on what seems to be working for others.

- **Use Etsy Stats**. Once your product has been listed for at least a month, Etsy stats can be a very powerful tool. You can view your shop data by clicking "Stats" in your Shop Manager. Or, in your "Listings" section, click on the arrow below each listing to see stats for that listing. Etsy will show you a list of keywords and phrases that have resulted in people visiting (clicking on) your item. These keywords and variations on them are great to include in your title if they're not already there, because they represent what actual customers have typed into Etsy's search box in searching for your product.

- **Using a Keyword Tool (Marmalead or eRank):** If you're ready to go a step beyond the free tools, a paid service can make writing titles and tags a lot easier and more efficient. These tools will show you how competitive a keyword is (how many other listings are using it), the search volume for each keyword (the number of people typing it into Etsy's search box each month), and the amount of engagement a keyword receives (how many people searching for that keyword or phrase actually click on listings and buys stuff).

- **Sign up for a Google AdWords account.** You don't actually have to USE Google Adwords. Just sign up for an account (it's very straightforward and easy) but don't create any ads. You'll have to put in payment information but you won't be charged. And then play around with the keyword tools within Google AdWords. You'll often find a whole slew of new keyword ideas this way that you hadn't thought of, and you'll be able to see how popular and competitive these keywords are.

The Bottom Line: Put your best keywords at the very front of your listing titles. Write straightforward titles using as many keywords with high engagement and low competition as you can fit within 140 characters.

Compelling Listing Attributes

When you go to Etsy.com, you'll notice that just under the search box are nine clickable categories—Everyday Finds, Jewelry & Accessories, Home & Living, etc. These are just the first level of categories that Etsy uses to divide and group the products across its enormous site. And there are hundreds of subcategories under each one. From a seller's perspective, these categories and subcategories are known as **attributes.**

In addition to browsing by category, customers can narrow their search results using **filters**. Here's how it works: After typing in something generic like "cool women's t-shirts," customers can check boxes listed down the left side of their results page. Like "blue," "free shipping," and "crew neck."

From a seller's perspective, you'll absolutely want to specify as many of your listing's attributes as possible. Why? Because you want your listing displayed in as many search categories and within as many filters as possible. Because each attribute you specify is a box that a potential customer may check when searching for a product *just like yours.*

Can you offer free shipping? *Check.* That's an incredibly valuable attribute because customers LOVE it and will often narrow their search just to find products that have it. Can you ship in one business day? *Check.* Is your product a specific color that fits into an attribute in Etsy's dropdown menu? Take advantage. Instead of listing your item's color as aqua, choose blue (because your potential customer doesn't have a filter option for aqua!). Another *check.* The more of these attribute filters you can feasibly pass through, the more likely you are to connect with the customer who wants exactly what you sell.

While Etsy's algorithm doesn't care how many or few attributes you list, it will still reward you for using them by putting your product in increasingly narrow search results (with less competition) if your product meets a customer's specific needs.

Choose the Right Product Category

Perhaps the most important attribute you'll select is your product category and subcategories (which is why they deserve their own subhead). When you do this, more attribute options related to this category will populate. It might look overwhelming to select all these attributes, but it's worth it! Painstakingly go through each set of options and select the ones that describe your product—but ONLY the ones that actually describe it. You don't have to, nor do you want to select an attribute for every single category proffered by Etsy (more on that in the next section). For now, just know that if an attribute definitely applies to your product (e.g., if you're selling a crew neck t-shirt and Etsy allows you to specify that), DO IT.

However, hold off on any categories or attributes that are confusing or ambiguous.

TIP: Follow Etsy's instructions for selecting a category by typing in a few descriptive words about your product, but don't just pick the first category Etsy suggests. Make sure you click the "manual" option, especially if you're a new seller. This will give you the option of selecting more specific subcategories related to your product. Fourth Wave's T-shirts, for example, are technically "women's t-shirts," which is the category Etsy always suggests when I create a new listing. However, manual selection allows me to choose a subcategory one level deeper, "women's graphic t-shirts," that better describes what I'm selling.

TIP: If you're not sure which category to pick or if more than one seems to fit, take a peek at what your top competitors are doing. There's a simple trick to spying on the competition—simply go to a listing that's similar to yours and also ranking well. Right-click anywhere on the page and select "view page source" from the dropdown menu. This will open up a new window with the html that makes up the page. If you "control + F" (find) and search for "tags" (with the quote marks), you'll be treated to a list of all the attributes and tags your competitor is using. The first of these will be the category.

Ignore Attributes That Don't Quite Fit

Some attributes are better than others. In fact, some attributes can actually hold you back and keep you OUT of search results.

Only select attributes that actually describe your product. For example, I have no doubt your crocheted cat sweater would be a really amazing Christmas present, but unless it's specifically a Christmas item, selecting "Christmas" under the holiday attribute list can end up limiting the number of people who see your item. It works like this: Customers have the power to limit the types of listings displayed to them by checking a box, and if that person has checked "Easter," Etsy will stop showing any item with a holiday attribute other than Easter. It will, however, keep showing items that have *no attribute* selected under "holiday," presumably because non-holiday specific items may still make great Easter gifts.

The Bottom Line: Carefully selected and accurate attributes are the clearest signals you can send to Etsy's search algorithm about what your product is and who your customers are. This process may seem tedious, but it's vital to a listing's success on Etsy's platform.

Include Variations When Needed

You can send positive or negative signals to Etsy's algorithm depending on how you use variations (if you use them, that is). Variations are very similar to attributes from Etsy's perspective. They make it easy to offer different sizes, colors, and styles of a product without listing each option as its own separate listings (saving you money!). However, if you do use variations, don't make them too complex, especially as a new seller. Your customers can be overwhelmed if you offer too many options. And like I mentioned before, if your variations are too unique, your listing will be thrown out of results any time a customer sets a filter.

But as with attributes, using Etsy's variations CAN help you rank higher in search if you use them properly. If you sell your product in several colors, make sure to use Etsy's "Color" variation option and pick the colors Etsy lists as options instead of creating your own (i.e., select "green" from the dropdown instead of creating a new variation called "forest"). That way, Etsy will show your product to the customers searching generic terms like "green women's t-shirt" as well as to customers who check "green" in the color filter.

Variations can be complicated to work with at first. Here's a step-by-step of how to set them up:

- Click on the variations button, and a pop-up will open. In this pop-up, you'll have the option of selecting a variation from a list provided by Etsy or creating your own.

- Depending on the variation you're using, you may also need to select a scale, for example, "US women's letter sizing."

- You can then add the options your customers will see by selecting from Etsy's generic list or by creating your own.

- You can choose two different variations and as many options under each as you want. (You'll only be able to link images to the first 10, though, and frankly, I'd recommend not offering more than 5-6 different colors or styles so as not to overwhelm your customers.)

Use Tags Wisely

Like titles, tags are a keyword-centric way to communicate with Etsy's algorithm. Etsy allows sellers 13 self-chosen tags per listing. Each tag can be a maximum of 20 characters in length. Because these tags are hidden from customers, it's tempting to treat them carelessly, especially since they're toward the bottom of the listing and decision fatigue is kicking in. You just want to be DONE.

Trust me, I know exactly how this feels. But remember, with online sales, you have to interact with customers through that pesky intermediary, the search algorithm, and tags are critically important to this. BUT, I have good news. You can use the same keywords (like the EXACT same ones) in your tags that you used in your title.

Here's how it works:

- Use all 13 tags available.

- As with your title, you'll want to use long-tail keyword phrases with high engagement and low competition whenever possible, and add generic, short-tail keywords if you have exhausted that long-tail list.

- Repeat the keywords from your title **exactly**. And use variations on the same keywords when you run out. Tell Etsy in your tags that your item is a "feminist shirt" and a "feminist t-shirt" as well as a "feminist tee shirt." (Remember, you're trying to think like a customer. How might different customers search for this item?)

- Within reason, the more times you include a certain keyword or phrase in different forms in your title and tags, the more convinced Etsy will be that your item fits that category and the higher it'll rank your item in results when a customer searches for the phrase "feminist shirt."

- The order of your tags doesn't matter. All 13 will be considered equally by the search algorithm.

- **Avoid** repeating the attributes you selected in your tags. Etsy gives extra ranking points to keywords repeated in both the *title* and the *tags*, but it sees tags and attributes as essentially the same thing, so repeating *attributes* in tags is wasted space.

- Recently, Etsy announced that its algorithm recognizes plurals, regional spellings, and misspellings in search queries, so including these variations in tags is also unnecessary. While I believe this is true for plurals ending in "s," well-recognized regional spelling differences (color vs. colour), and common misspellings and typos (coffe instead of coffee), if your product is quite unique or your industry very niche, you might want to include these keyword variants in your tags to be safe. In other words, it's not a hard "don't," but it might save you some space in your tags for more important keywords.

- Don't adjust tags more often than every 30 days. It takes about this long for changes to take effect and for sellers to see results in Etsy stats.

TIP #1: If a long-tail keyword phrase is too long to fit in one tag, it's perfectly acceptable to split it across 2 or more tags. Just repeat the most important keywords. For example, Fourth Wave get's a lot of traffic from the long-tail phrase "trendy plus size clothing," which doesn't fit in a single tag. I break it into two tags "trendy plus size" and "plus size clothing."

TIP #2: Tags are hidden from customers, so you can include loosely related recognizable words and phrases here that might get you views but that you might not want to have in your title (cheat words). Examples include Shop Names of your Etsy competitors who get a lot of views for similar items, pop-culture references and hashtags that a customer might type into a search box when they don't know exactly what they're looking for product-wise, and trademarked words and phrases (be extra careful with this last one).

WARNING! The practices mentioned in Tip #2 technically fall under the category of black hat (or at least gray) SEO—basically, they try to trick the search algorithm into displaying listings it wouldn't normally display for a particular search. And just as Google is cracking down on the black-hat SEO techniques used in the early 2000s, Etsy's algorithm will probably get wiser in the coming years. In other words, manipulating your tags *does* work in the 2020s (I confess, I do it), but it may not work forever.

The Bottom Line: Fill in the tags as much as possible with the best keywords from your title. Then wait 30 days, and hone the tags to reflect what your customers are searching for that gets them buying your product.

Finding the BEST Tags

The process for finding the best tags is the same as choosing keywords for your title, so you can use all the tools we talked about in the Title section. These tools will help you get inside the minds of your customers, to know exactly what they are searching for and what they're actually buying.

I highly recommend using a service like Marmalead or eRank to make choosing tags as painless and efficient as possible, but you can absolutely create an amazing listing without a paid service. It just might take a little more work and experimentation.

Etsy's Obsession with Seasons/Trends

Along with choosing tags and keywords that describe your product, you'll want to choose some tags and keywords related to the "season" in which you think it'll most likely sell. "But my product isn't seasonal," I hear you say, "It's popular year round." That may be technically true in the real world, but Etsy has an obsession with seasonality. They refer to it as "trends," but I prefer the term "seasons" because that better describes the search algorithm's behavior.

Etsy's algorithm gives boosts in rank to listings that were trending during certain weeks or months in previous years. Thus, you might discover an old listing is doing really well again in the fall of 2020 even though the trend for that product really happened in the fall of 2019.

As far as I can tell, seasonality is a ranking factor that is unique to Etsy, at least to the degree that it affects ranking. At the tip of the iceberg, seasonality is just what it sounds like: At Christmas, Etsy gives a ranking boost to listings with "Christmas" tags, attributes, and titles. This makes sense—more people are searching for Christmas items—but Etsy goes even further and ranks Christmas items higher during the Christmas season even for searches that don't relate to Christmas. For example, if you sell a Christmas-themed baby blanket, and someone searches for "baby blankets" in December, Etsy will boost your listing right to the top because of the season, even if it wouldn't rank high normally for such a generic keyword.

Etsy also uses your sales data from previous years to determine when your listings might be popular again in the current year and gives them an automatic rank boost during those same days or weeks they sold well in years past. What this does is it gives "seasonality" to listings that aren't seasonal at all. For example, after the 2018 State of the Union Address, Fourth Wave sold a shirt depicting Nancy Pelosi clapping with the phrase "Clappity Clap" above her head. The shirt got picked up by BuzzFeed in an article on the "most sarcastic shirts of the week." We sold over 600 shirts in a few short weeks in June that year. This incredible conversion rate sent a lot of positive signals to Etsy, and the next June, 2019, Etsy bumped that listing to the top again for searches like "Feminist shirt" and "trendy plus size clothing" and other more generic keywords. We joked that the shirt was selling well again because it was "Nancy Pelosi season."

In practical terms for your shop, the concept of seasonality can be used to make sure you have a steady flow of items selling throughout the year, even if your stuff isn't particularly seasonal in the traditional holiday or weather sense. Take a listing that's not already selling super well at a particular time of year, and think outside the box—would your item be a good Mother's Day gift? Change a tag or two at the beginning of April to "Mother's Day gift" related keywords. If an item really takes off during the "Mother's Day buying season," don't change the tag. Etsy will still display your item throughout the year, but it'll give it an even bigger boost in ranking next Mother's Day. If you can make sure you have items that fit a "season" throughout the year, you'll have a good steady flow of income even if it looks like certain items have stopped selling while others are taking off. Seasons can be anything—graduation, summer, winter, pop culture references (e.g., Fortnite season, Joe Exotic season—we had a lot of fun with that one).

The Bottom Line: Over the course of your first year selling on Etsy, keep track of which items sell well at certain times of the year. If you sell a lot of a product in the spring and summer, consider adding listings specifically targeted to fall and winter seasons so you have steady product sales all year round. Read over Etsy's yearly "Trend Report" for ideas on seasons to target (Google "Etsy Trend Report" for the current year's findings).

Hone Your Listing Descriptions

Etsy's search algorithm doesn't currently look at the listing description at all when determining where your listing should rank for a given search. This means that if your goal is to sell your product on Etsy's platform only, you can keep your description brief, geared toward your customer, and focus your SEO efforts on your title, attributes, and tags.

So, are listing descriptions unimportant? Nope! Here's why:

Anatomy of a Good Listing Description

A good description is still important.

1. It can help your customers connect with your product or shop —Etsy customers don't just want to know about the item they're buying, they want to know about you. As a small seller on Etsy's handmade mom-and-pop online platform, you have the opportunity not only to offer a one-of-a-kind product but to build up a base of customers loyal to you and to your shop. You also have the opportunity to fully describe your product and preemptively answer your customer's questions (We dig into a deep discussion about the importance of copy and good listing descriptions more in Book 2).

2. While Etsy doesn't look at your listing description, Google does. Google's search algorithm "reads" the first 150 characters of your listing description to determine when and where to rank it. This means that a well-written description can help your listing rank in Google search results and reach a much wider audience.

The First 150 Characters of Your Description

Unlike Etsy, Google does not look kindly on keyword stuffing, so write your description in readable sentences as you would if you were writing directly to your customer. Make sure to include relevant keywords within your beautiful prose, especially in the first 150 characters. Just as you did in researching keywords for Etsy search, researching high-volume, low competition keywords for Google will give your listing the best chance at ranking in a Google search. Tools like Google AdWords' "Keyword Planner" and the Chrome extension "Keywords Everywhere" can help you do this.

Don't copy and paste the same or a very similar description into several listings. Come up with something fresh. Google's search algorithm flags and penalizes duplication when it finds it, so even if you sell many products that are very similar to one another, write a new description for each one focusing on different keywords in each. If you're finding your listings are so similar that it's difficult if not impossible to come up with varying descriptions, you may want to consider consolidating all of these products under a single listing by taking advantage of the Etsy's options for listing variations.

Additional Product Information

After the first 150 characters (usually the first sentence or two (if they're short)), give customers more information about your product, stuff that's not obvious when looking at the listing images. Do customers have the option to get the item monogrammed? Does your product have a scent? Tell customers about the history of your product. What inspired the design? Are you donating proceeds to a cause? This is the kind of information that makes a great description and connects you to your customers well beyond a single sale.

Information about Your Shop and Yourself

After giving a description of your product, give your customers some basic information about your shop. Hit the highlights. Your shop's "About" and "Shop Policies" sections are better places for lots of details. Direct customers to these sections and to your FAQ if they have questions. You can even include links to these pages. Etsy doesn't currently allow linked text, but you can shorten extremely long links using Bitly.com and paste the shortened links into your description. You can also link to similar products if you have any. And ask customers to sign up for your mailing list if you have one.

Direct Them to Your Social Channels

Either just before your shop information or at the end of your description, direct customers to your social channels: "Find us on Facebook and Instagram @YourCompanyName." I explain in depth how to maximize the benefit from social channels in Book 2, but for now, let's just agree that social is key to marketing in today's world.

Example Description

First 150 characters ⌐⌐

Rhinoceros grocery tote, "Head up, stay strong." Great gift for that friend having a hard time. Help save the planet one shopping trip at a time with this large, reusable 100% cotton grocery tote. © Design by Fourth Wave Feminist Apparel

Useful information ⌐⌐

Totes are 11 x 13 inches and sturdy enough to hold a lot more groceries than plastic bags.

Looking for something a little different? Explore the rest of our grocery totes!

Link to our homepage ⌐↓

https://www.etsy.com/shop/fourthwaveapparel

Fourth Wave feminist apparel makes a great gift for your favorite sister in the resistance, ally, friend, or partner. Or, you know, yourself.

Where we donate ⌐↓

5% of all profits are donated to the Thurgood Marshall College Fund, which earns an incredible 100% rating on Charity Navigator for its effective work in helping students at HBCUs (historically black colleges and universities) and predominantly black institutions through leadership, lobbying, job recruiting, and scholarships.

We have a FAQ ⌐↓

Check out our FAQ for more information on custom order, organizations we donate to, sizing, materials, shipping, and wholesale opportunities.

Find us on social channels ⌐↓

Find us on Facebook, Pinterest, and Instagram!
@FourthWaveApparel

Etsy's Point System for Listings

It's important to understand that Etsy's algorithm is always at work. And it's always evaluating your shop as a whole as well as your individual listings. Remember that "shop quality score"? Well, Etsy also gives a point value to each of your listings, and this "listing quality score" has far-reaching effects. It impacts where each of your listings rank individually, and the average of your listing quality scores is also a factor Etsy uses to determine your shop quality score. This means Etsy's algorithm punishes (drops in rank) poor listings twice over—once for the low quality of the listing and again for a low shop quality score. But this also means a shop full of awesome listings will be rewarded handsomely.

Here's the details. For each listing in your shop, Etsy awards an ever-changing number of points (the listing quality score) that determines where it ranks in comparison to similar listings. New listings start at zero points and, as time goes on, earn or lose points depending largely on the *conversion rate* (the ratio of views to sales) of the individual listing.

Imagine you've listed your item as a "dog sweater" because it's an adult-size sweater with a picture of a dog on it. The problem is that most people searching for "dog sweater" want a sweater *for a dog* rather than one for a human. Your dog sweater listing will likely get a lot of *impressions* (views) at first, especially because Etsy gives a boost in rank to new listings. But as time goes on, and almost nobody searching for "dog sweater" *engages with* (clicks on) let alone buys your sweater, your conversion rate will drop and Etsy will punish the listing with a negative listing quality score.

Listings with negative scores rank more poorly in search results for all relevant searches. And this listing can drag your shop down with it. It might only be one tag that's causing you problems, but if you have one problematic tag, none of the rest of your carefully chosen tags will be serving you fully. In this case, the best strategy is to deactivate (remove) the listing and relist the item (as a completely new listing) without the problematic keyword, in this case "dog sweater."

Some Etsy sellers are rumored to repost *many or all of their listings every day* in order to "reset" them and take advantage of the temporary boost in rank given to new listings. This seems more like rumor than fact to me, and it's certainly not necessary or even advisable for a seller trying to do well on Etsy. Plus, who has time for that? Not me.

Guidance for When to List, Renew, Edit, and Take Down Listings

Etsy loves sellers who are highly involved. Good sellers (aka, involved sellers) give Etsy a good reputation as a platform, which is why Etsy has written its search algorithm to reward sellers who interact regularly with their shops.

New and Renewed Listings Get a Boost in Rank

New listings and renewed listings tell Etsy a seller is engaging with her shop. And the algorithm gives a temporary but significant boost in rank to all new and renewed listings. This doesn't mean that your new listings will automatically appear on the first page for those high-competition keywords. Etsy still places a listing in results based on other ranking factors first (including relevancy and shop quality score); then, from there, it bumps it up a number of positions (it's impossible to give an exact number here, so let's just say a *noticeable* number, sometimes a full page or more!). This is also true for renewed listings, by which I mean listings that have been automatically renewed by Etsy (which happens every four months), manually renewed by the seller, or renewed after a sale (on items with a quantity of more than one).

What does this look like exactly? For Fourth Wave, the temporary rank boost for renewed listings means that certain designs sell in waves. A customer will purchase our "phenomenal woman" shirt after a general search for "feminist shirts," and because a sale causes the listing to renew, Etsy's algorithm will temporarily boost that shirt for all searches related to "feminist shirts," which means more customers will see it and buy it. That week, we'll have an unusual number of sales of the "phenomenal woman" design before it drops back down in the results.

TIP: Remember that this boost in rank is only temporary (1-2 hours if that), so if you plan to add a new listing, try to do it when the maximum number of your customers will be online. For Etsy's overall platform, this is 9:30–11:30 am Eastern time, but it will, of course, vary seller to seller, so be sure to check your stats and post new listings during the hours your customers are most likely to see them.

The Bottom Line: Etsy rewards sellers who regularly add new listings and renew old ones.

Deactivating Listings for a Better Conversion Rate

In the Tags section, I discuss how Etsy uses the *conversion rate* (number of sales divided by the number of views) of a listing to determine that listing's rank in search results. In addition to looking at the conversion rate of the individual listing it's displaying, Etsy's algorithm also looks at a shop's overall conversion rate for the last 30 days and rewards or punishes all the listings in a shop based on that number.

A good conversion rate on Etsy is about 3-4%, so we're not talking very big numbers here. The amazing news is that it's shockingly easy to improve your conversion rate. We've done it with great success. If you're in the 1% range, you may want to try some of the ideas below to bring it up just a few percentage points. Credit for many of these ideas goes to Joanna Vaughan, a writer for the Marmalead Blog and an absolute wizard at Etsy SEO. Definitely check out her tutorials for more tips and ideas.

- Deactivate listings that aren't selling well. The criteria for "not selling well" will be something you'll want to determine up front. For Fourth Wave, I decided to flag all listings that had had fewer than two sales in the last year. I also flagged low-margin items (aka, we don't make much from a sale anyway) that had fewer than six sales in the same time. With these items gone from the shop, customers more often saw and purchased the already popular listings, and our conversion rate jumped.

- Set up a "Last Chance Sale." Thanks Joanna for this brilliant advice. Instead of immediately deactivating all the items you flagged as not selling well, place these items into their own section called "Last Chance" or "Clearance," and discount them at least 25-30% for a month before deactivating them. This can really get sluggish listings selling again. Customers *love* a sale as does Etsy's search algorithm, and the "last chance" element also prompts customers to impulse buy, since they know these products are disappearing after the sale.

The Bottom Line: Keeping a close eye on your stats can help you see which listings are selling and which aren't. And either getting rid of or discounting listings that aren't selling can really bump up your shop's conversion rate, which improves the rank of all the listings in your shop.

Another great way to send "involved seller" signals to Etsy's algorithm is to regularly interact with your existing listings. This can be in small ways—changes like swapping out an image, replacing a keyword with another, or editing your listing title or description. You'll want to rotate through your listings when doing this; Etsy recommends you leave a listing alone for 30 days after any changes to give the algorithm time to recognize the changes and recalculate the listing's rank in search results. And don't ever make any major changes to your best sellers. You don't want to break what's already working. The goal with regular fine-tuning is less to achieve the PERFECT listing and more to show Etsy that you're a good investment because you really care about your shop and are highly engaged in its success. After all, your success is Etsy's success as well.

Stuff We Learned the Hard Way

When it comes to creating superb listings, I've learned more than I'd like to admit the hard way. I started out using whimsical product names in my titles, picking unrelated tags that felt right just to fill space, copy-pasting my listing descriptions, and so much more. I'd like to list some of my biggest ah-ha moments, so you don't have to make the same mistakes I did.

Keywords: When I first started making listings, I used as wide a range of keywords as you could imagine from "feminist shirt" to "hipster tee" to keywords related specifically to the design like "steamroller" and "bloomers." I used up the title space and continued filling the tags with ever more obscure words and phrases. My listings definitely got a lot of views that way. The problem was that the people seeing my listings were usually looking for something else entirely, so I had a terrible conversion rate.

I finally discovered that I should have been putting the *exact same keywords* in both my titles and tags. And I should have picked the strongest 5-6 keywords and filled in the rest of the space with variations on these same keywords.

Cannibalizing an old listing for a new product: Just don't do it. I'll tell you I used to do this all the time simply because it saved me time. Because creating new listings takes a LOT of time. There are two main problems with just recycling an existing listing for a new product. One, the new product will be "tainted" by the sales (or lack of sales) from the old one. (Remember Etsy's point system and the listing quality score?) Odds are, if you're replacing one product with another, the old product wasn't selling very well, which means it has accrued a lot of negative ranking points from Etsy's algorithm. This starts the new listing off at a huge disadvantage, and you miss out on the rank boost Etsy gives to new listings.

Two, your stats for that listing have become largely worthless. The conversion rate over time is meaningless because it averages the sales and views of both products, and the keywords the listing is being found for are mixed between the old and new products. It's not impossible to separate, but it's way more trouble than it's worth. Trust me on this one.

Selecting attributes that don't exactly describe your product: For at least a year, I had our "phenomenal woman" shirt listed as a Valentine's Day item (E.g., I checked this box as an attribute). The design is in the shape of a heart, after all, and the shirt did sell in February. But it completely stopped selling the rest of the year until I finally unchecked the Valentine's Day box. All of a sudden, the shirt started showing up in searches throughout the year. I honestly had no idea how detrimental limiting my listing in that way would be. The takeaway is that if you're unsure an attribute really describes your product well, it's probably wise to leave it blank. Your item may still experience seasonal highs and lows—and certainly don't be afraid to list season keywords in your title and tags! But be VERY careful about checking those holiday boxes. Go ahead and experiment but make sure you do some testing over several months to see if the listing actually benefits from being categorized a certain way by Etsy or not.

CHAPTER 3

Product Photography and Listing Images

We've already established that LISTINGS are the heart of your Etsy shop as far as Etsy's algorithm is concerned. And as far as your customers are concerned, too. Because without listings, you can't make sales.

Product photography and listing images, then, are one of the most critical parts of your listing. Because overwhelmingly, Etsy customers report that they determine whether or not to click on a product based on its image. And you'd better believe that those customer signals are important to Etsy's algorithm (not to mention your own sales).

What I'm trying to say is this: I can't really overstate the importance of good product photography. The image your buyer sees as they scroll through Etsy search results is often your one shot at a first impression. Think of it like Tinder. Your goal is to get your potential buyer to STOP scrolling, forget the competition, and think, "WHOA, I want to get to know THAT soap dish/custom ant farm/ pair of socks better.

Much like Tinder, if you don't stand out, have boring or off-putting listing images, or don't represent yourself accurately and favorably, you're not going to get a second glance, let alone a date.

And at this point you might find yourself thinking "But I'm not a graphic designer, I don't know how to use photoshop, I only have a basic smartphone, and I should give up because I don't have the technical skills to do this." I want you to stop it right now. We're going to talk about graphics and design (and the tools you can use and master and look like a legit PRO even if you don't know what a pixel is yet). That's coming up in Chapter 4. For right now, let's talk about best practices for the images you're going to create with your blossoming photography skills.

First, Let's Get a Few Things Straight

If you're new to Etsy (or if you're just new to Etsy lingo), it can get a little confusing when we talk about different image types. So let's start with a few definitions.

Some of the tips I'm going to share with you are specific to **main images.** (I'll also refer to them as **"thumbnail images.")** Main images are the very first image any buyer will see BEFORE they click on your product in an Etsy search. That main image will appear as a little thumbnail image alongside competitors' items when your buyer is scrolling through Etsy search results, looking for something that meets their needs. If a buyer clicks on the thumbnail image, they'll be taken to your product page, where they'll see an expanded/larger version of that thumbnail image. In other words, main images/thumbnail images are extra important.

When I talk about **listing images**, I'm referring to all ten images that your potential buyers will see when they click on a particular listing. There's your main image and nine **product images**. These ten images are important and help seal the deal with a buyer. But remember, your buyer will only be able to scroll through all ten photos AFTER you've successfully enticed them to click on your product through that all-important main image.

Best Practices for Photography on Etsy

Remember how I told you that Etsy buyers consistently point to images as the most important factor in whether or not they engage with your products? Well, here's some data: In a survey conducted by Etsy itself, 9 out of 10 Etsy buyers indicated that listing images were the main factor that determined whether or not they made a purchase. That's a BIG deal.

So, what goes into good images on Etsy? Whether we're talking about a main/thumbnail image or a product image, there's some very important best practices that apply to any image you use.

First, a few boring technical tips:

- **Your listing images should be 2,000 pixels wide.** This size looks best for desktop and mobile users. Etsy WILL let you upload images that are narrower than 2,000 pixels, but they aren't going to look nearly as good.

- **Images should be 75-dpi JPEGs.** Do take the time to set your image resolution to 75 dpi so your images are both screen viewable and not too large to upload. And make sure they're in .jpg format. (Etsy will accept PNGs and GIFs, but doesn't upload these as reliably.)

- **Make all of your listing images the same shape.** Use a 4:3 ratio (basically a fat rectangle) for optimal viewing experience (this also allows you to zoom and crop your thumbnail preview for buyers, but shows the entire product with some white space once the buyer clicks on it.)

- **Include your logo and Shop Name in a visible but unobtrusive place in each photo.** This helps your potential buyers recognize your shop as a distinct entity. (Sometimes folks tend to see Etsy as one big store instead of many different small shops.) Some people also choose to watermark (overlay a transparent logo) over their photos to deter copyright thieves from stealing their photos. (We'll talk more about copyright in Chapter 7.)

That's the technical stuff you need to know. Now on to the fun stuff:

- **Make sure your photographs are in focus.** This might sound like a no-brainer, but if it was so obvious, I wouldn't see so many slightly blurry photos on Etsy. Take your photos in good lighting, and prop your phone or camera up with a stand or against a solid surface to minimize jitter from your hands. Don't tell yourself it's "not a big deal" if the image is just a LITTLE blurry. Blurriness equates with sloppiness and amateur hour in your buyer's mind. Use crisp photos.

- **As Lizzo puts it, you need the "bomb lighting."** Natural light (from the sun) is ideal, but that isn't always easy. You're looking for soft, diffused lighting that you find in the hour before sunset or after sunrise. Avoid harsh shadows and blown-out highlights. If natural lighting is too difficult to achieve, take your photos indoors in a well-lit room (from natural sunlight). Experiment with different angles and different times of day to get the best results. The time you spend will be worth it.

- **Invest in basic equipment.** If you're selling small items, do yourself a favor and purchase a cheap light box (you can find one easily on Amazon). It'll give you perfect lighting and excellent results with minimal effort. If you have larger items, invest in a lighting kit and photo backdrops. If you have the perfect natural environment that you can use as a backdrop with excellent lighting, that's amazing. But consider whether that natural photo studio will be available to you year-round whenever you need to photograph. If it isn't, create a photo nook that will allow you to replicate your listing photos (particularly your main/thumbnail images) year-round, with a consistent result.

- **Don't be coy with your buyers.** Show exactly what the product is, and keep it very simple, e.g., if you are selling ceramic pots, don't show a ceramic pot sitting in a saucer beside a cute watering can. Keep the main focus on your product. If you have too much going on in your photos, you're going to confuse or annoy your buyers, who imagine they will have to do some digging to figure out what you're actually selling.

- **Use props wisely and sparingly.** Despite the importance of keeping the focus on your products, props can be an invaluable tool to show size and context. Make sure your props serve a purpose and don't distract from your product but instead give additional information about your item (like how it's used, its relative size to something your buyer will be familiar with, or how it might look displayed).

- **Give your buyers accurate, easy-to-interpret information.** This should include information about color, size, shape, and texture. You don't want to send mixed messages about any of these things. Back this visual information up with your listing description.

- **Define your shop's holistic style.** You might want to create a vision board on Pinterest or just cut photos out of magazines that appeal to you and deliver the tone and feel that you want your buyers to see when they look at your images and your shop as a whole. This is hugely important to creating a cohesive shop (your buyers will interpret this as professionalism and skill in your craft). For instance, if you have some photos that are peaceful, with white backgrounds and succulents, don't suddenly throw in images that are filled with splashes of bright color and funky wallpaper. This creates a disjointed feeling when a buyer looks at your shop as a whole or peruses through additional listings. Here's some ways you can achieve that consistency:

- o **Use simple, consistent backdrops for your products.** I recommend choosing 3-4 backdrops and reusing them over and over again. These backdrops can be different and unique, but they must look cohesive and beautiful next to each other.

- o **Come up with a color and texture palette that you adhere to in your images.** This doesn't mean everything you post HAS to be in those colors. But hone in on a few key colors and textures that you tie into everything you do, whether that's whitewashed fences, neutral burlap, rustic brown wood, leafy green plants, neon vases, etc. Keep it consistent, and be intentional about the colors and patterns that appear throughout your shop.

- **Consider seasonality and style trends**. If you have a big shop, it may be a lot of work to update listing photos with seasonally enticing colors and options. However, it may be worth the effort to essentially put a big red bow on your best sellers that shine during Christmas or to have summer and winter photos of your product that you change out twice a year. This will communicate relevance to your buyers. I tend to choose a somewhat neutral palette for most of my image backgrounds and color palettes, but I do update these images every year or so to help my shop look fresh instead of dated.

Main images (Thumbnail Images): Your First Priority for Photography

If you get only one listing image perfect, make it your thumbnail image. I know you have limited hours in a day, and you're likely juggling a lot of roles as a shop owner. So, it's important to prioritize your efforts. Main images (thumbnail images) deserve your first priority. Main images are the image buyers will see as they scroll through your shop, or more often the wild world of Etsy search results when they type in a query.

For the most part, your thumbnail image should be a simple, clean studio shot that shows the product itself up close. A white background or very clean, simple background is optimal. This image should show your buyer exactly what they will be buying. The image should be clean and bright, crisp and beautiful. This is the virtual equivalent of your buyer seeing the product on a shelf and saying, "Oooh, look at that!"

Product images

In addition to your main image are the nine product images in any given listing.

All of the product images you include in addition to your main image/thumbnail image are important to sealing the deal with a buyer and communicating proficiency and thoroughness to Etsy's algorithms. Which is why it's critical that you maximize all ten listing images to give your buyer a complete picture. Etsy shows you different thumbnails in the open image slots, encouraging you to show your product from different angles, illustrate its size and texture, where it was created, who might love it, and how it might be used. Here's a breakdown of the image shots I recommend you include:

- **Lifestyle:** Include one or two shots that look like a sneak peek into someone's home or life after purchasing your product. These lifestyle shots may show your product being displayed (on someone's wall, shelf, or closet), enjoyed, or interacted with (e.g., children playing with a toy, people having a snowball fight in your hat, or a couple cuddled up under your minky blanket reading a story). Lifestyle photos allow your buyer to see themselves using and interacting with your product.

- **Genesis and creation:** If you make your product by hand (or someone else does), lean into that handmade vibe (remember, your buyers are on Etsy for a reason), and show the product being created. Show your buyer the thing that you'd show them if they came to visit your studio—the most interesting and fun-looking aspect of creation, e.g., you working with fire, or saws, or inky screens, or sewing in your amazing artsy craft room.

- **Options:** If your buyer will need to make choices about color, size, style, etc., it's a really smart idea to show those variations side by side in a matrix-type image. This helps your buyer feel prepared to make these choices when they add your product to their cart instead of wondering, "Wait, what is blue vs. aqua? What sizing scale is this?" While you should certainly communicate information about options and sizing in your listing description and variations, many people will look at images for this kind of information without reading your descriptions very thoroughly. Use this opportunity to instill confidence and provide details visually.

- **Model shots:** If your product can be worn or displayed on a person, FIND YOURSELF A MODEL AND PHOTOGRAPH THEM. This doesn't need to be an expensive endeavor. You may have friends or family willing to model, or you may be able to find models who are excited to be part of your shoot in exchange for products, etc. You can also model your products yourself, as long as you can find someone to take the photo for you (or use a self-timer on your phone). Choose models that resemble your target market and customer. Play around with different poses and backgrounds for your model shots, and pay attention to the way an urban, natural, or indoor setting jives with the vibe and colors you're working toward cohesively creating in your shop.

- **Visual scale shot:** For most products, your buyer will want to have a very clear idea of exactly how big it is. While this information should be provided to your buyer in exact measurements in your listing description, you should also give your buyer a clear idea of scale by showing the product in context and next to easily recognizable objects, e.g., show earrings next to a quarter, in the palm of your hand, or on someone's earlobe.

- **Accessories and companion items:** Do you sell accessories or companion items that your buyer might love (if only they knew about them?!). Use one of your listing photos to advertise to an interested buyer (who is invested enough in your products to spend time scrolling through your listing) additional products they might love. Buyers who are ready to make a purchase are likely to add an extra item to their cart from your shop if they're inspired by what they see/encouraged to explore the rest of your shop. Since many buyers will be introduced to your shop by a single listing they click on in Etsy search (and may not even see your shop as a whole), it's important to entice them to look around.

- **Fine details and textures:** Don't count on your buyers to zoom in to inspect tiny details, textures, and other little things that they might easily glance past on their phone. Zoomed-in images help you avoid returns and surprises for your buyer that can result in bad reviews. It also helps you show the fine craftsmanship and detail that sets your item apart from other competitors.

Do you use one listing to sell a product that comes in several colors, sizes, or varieties? If so, you can add variations for up to two attributes (e.g., size, dimensions, color, or style).

Once you've set your variations, you can link photos from your main 10 to those variations. This functionally means that your thumbnail/main image will vary depending on what your buyer searches for (i.e., if they search for a blue dress and you've listed "blue" as a color variation and linked a photo, that photo of your blue dress will show up in search for your buyer instead of the red dress you've set as your main image).

Taking advantage of variation photos can help you connect with motivated buyers who have something very specific in mind. For instance, if a buyer is searching for a red dress and your image of a white dress appears in search, that buyer may scroll past (even though you have a red dress available). An immediate visual match to a specific search query helps snag a motivated buyer.

Stuff We Learned the Hard Way about Photography

Because images are so important and so unique to each business, there's going to be some trial and error. We certainly have had our share of lessons learned, and I'm sure we'll continue to refine. Here's some of the big stuff we learned the hard way:

Zoom Issues: For a while, I operated under the impression that buyers needed to see every single inch of my product—which meant that my thumbnail/main listing images looked small. And as it turns out, we got a LOT more sales once we zoomed in a little bit more so that buyers could more easily see our designs (the most important part of a shirt in many respects) clearly and easily as they scrolled. Once the buyer clicked, of course, they were able to see my main image in all its glory and white space. But to entice that click, I needed to zoom in more. Experiment with zoom, and you might be surprised by how it affects your sales.

Using lifestyle shots as the main image: Lifestyle shots are so beautiful and so compelling. They just FEEL like Etsy, right? So we used them as our main images for way too long before realizing that those clean, bright studio shots sold way more stuff. Why? Probably because they weren't as busy; it was clear to someone scrolling past what we were selling. And maybe those clean studio shots are more similar to what a buyer is used to seeing in other online shopping venues. Those lifestyle shots are very important. But use them as your main image with caution, and don't say I didn't warn you.

Being inconsistent in our global presentation: As our shop started to grow, it felt hard to wrangle that overall aesthetic—which meant that sometimes, because of entropy, our shop didn't look very cohesive. Colors weren't harmonizing, some photos looked like they belonged in an entirely different shop, and so on. It took some TIME to get this right, but it was worth it. We have a far more professional presentation and aesthetic nowadays, and we're taken more seriously because of it.

Not communicating enough visually: I'm a reader and a detail person. When I personally purchase something, I read every single word of the listing description. But that's me. And it was a hard lesson to learn that not everybody does this. Most scan through photos, scan for any questions they might have, and make a purchase. I've learned not to assume buyers will read my listing descriptions, and to communicate a lot of info about sizing, color options, fit, etc., in one of my listing images to increase the chances that buyers will order the correct item that meets their needs (and not return it to me or give me a negative review).

CHAPTER 4

Graphics and Design

Not all of the images you use in your shop will be plain photographs. Often, you'll want to use photographs with text, images with text, graphics, and infographics to communicate information with your customers visually. You'll use design elements in your shop banner, shop updates, social media, and within your listings. In other words, it's pretty important to understand the basic principles of design and how to create graphics.

If you haven't already read the previous chapter about listing images (Chapter 3), go back and read it first, even if you have no idea what a pixel is and you're feeling ANXIETY because the idea of trying to create beautiful images and graphics for your shop seems beyond your grasp. Don't worry, we've got you covered.

That's what this chapter is about. You don't need to have a degree in graphic design or even an artistic predisposition to create beautiful images for your shop. (But for real, go back and read Chapter 3 first. You need to know where you're headed before we talk about how to get there.)

We'll be covering best practices for design in your Etsy shop, advice for beginners, tools that are easy for just about anyone to master, and color theory too (how to use colors to appeal to your customers). We'll also touch on photographs again since they play such an important role in many design elements you'll create for your shop.

First, Some Advice for Noobs

If you're just starting out on Etsy (or haven't really dipped your toe into the designable elements of your shop just yet), let me offer a few bits of advice about design before we dive right in:

Figure Out Your Style

Spend a lot of time looking at other Etsy shops, other online shops (not necessarily Etsy), and the types of images that grab your eye when you're cruising through social media. Start a Google drive or a private Pinterest board of the ones that stand out to you. You don't have to know why they stand out to you yet, you just need to recognize that someone did a fantastic job of catching your interest, drawing your eye, or making you think, "Oooh, I need that in my life!" This is going to give you a much better idea of your own personal style. Do you gravitate toward bold colors and fonts? Feminine, delicate details? Playful images?

Put Your Style into Words

After you've gathered your collection of images, create a style sheet for your shop. Include your five favorite images (basically, make yourself a little collage of the stuff that appeals to you the very most), and then write keywords that describe the style that you want to embrace, e.g.:

Bold, dramatic colors, serious models, cacti accents.

Or

Playful, rainbow colors, silly models, lots of polka dots

This might sound like a school assignment, but it'll help you nail down your style in words so you can duplicate it across your shop.

Choose a Color Palette

If you're not sure what to do here, google the phrase "color palettes," and then pull a few that you like. These are colors that look good together/complement each other and can be used over and over in elements of your images and photos to keep things cohesive.

I'd recommend you choose about five or six colors that look great together. That's not to say you can't incorporate other colors into your shop—but make these colors the meat and potatoes of your appearance and your design elements.

Join a Facebook group or Etsy Forum for Feedback

Find a group that's supportive, intended for Etsy or small business owners to bounce ideas off each other, and share your ideas. Don't worry about sounding silly. But as you create initial attempts at cover photos, social media images, and product main images, you'll be amazed by how useful feedback from your peers can be—and how little feedback you actually need to get a good consensus of what a larger audience might think. Five to ten people's opinions, and you'll get a good idea of whether something is working or not (and why). This feedback is an extra step in your process of creating graphics, but it will save you time in the long run as you hone in on what works (and why).

Elements of Successful Graphics and Images

So, what makes a good graphic or image? The first element is CONTEXT (Which is why I'm going to again recommend that you go back and read Chapter 3 on listing images). The most technically beautiful photo of a bunch of employees enjoying their morning coffee isn't going to sell your office humor mugs. A simple studio shot is (as your main image, anyway. You should definitely include that employee photo as one of the other nine!).

That said, the other half of a successful photo or graphic is the technical stuff. The stuff that, if you saw the photo or graphic outside any kind of context would make you either nod your head and say, "That's a good photo," or shake your head and think, "Amateur hour." In this chapter, we're mostly dealing with the technical aspect. So, let's talk about what makes a good photo or graphic:

Elements of Successful Graphics

You'll use graphics heavily in your social media channels to communicate with customers and potential buyers about your brand, your style, news from your shop, etc. You'll also use graphics on Etsy when you post shop updates, and sometimes within listing photos to communicate details about sizing, color options, etc.

Good graphics vary in style, color, font choices, and composition. But good graphics all follow these design rules:

Keep it Simple

The number one mistake of new designers is using too many different fonts, too many images, and too much text. Basically, too much clutter. Most of the time, you have one fleeting moment to attract your buyer's attention on social media, ads, or your news feed on Etsy. Don't confuse or overwhelm them with too much information or the equivalent of a confetti cannon.

The Less Text the Better, Generally

And the fewer fonts the better, generally. If you're new at this, some of the tools listed below (in "Tools You Should Master") include templates meant just for you—basically, someone else has already done the work of pairing compatible fonts, colors, and layouts.

Take a Page from the Pros

Stick closely to the templates in graphics programs like Canva until you understand better why certain formats and fonts work well together, a.k.a., don't trust your eyes at first. Starting out in graphic design can be a lot of fun, and once you know enough to be dangerous, you may be tempted to ride without training wheels a little too quickly. I made the same mistake, and I look back on some of my earliest creations and ... they weren't awesome.

Keep it Balanced

Does one side of your image have a lot of text while there's a lot of blank space on the other side? In other words, is it too heavy or light on one side or the other? You want to create a feeling of balance within your graphics.

Keep it Aligned

You also want to create a sense of alignment by positioning design elements like text, borders, and blammies* in relationship with one another instead of haphazardly. Alignment creates a sense of order instead of chaos. The basic types of alignment include left or right alignment (elements that align along the left or right side of the image) and centered alignment (elements that are centered in the middle of the image). Basically, create an imaginary line running along the left, right, or center of the page and make sure the edges of your text and images touch that line to create a feeling of order. It's okay to use a couple of different types of alignment in one image, as long as you're consistent. For example, you might center the heading and subheading, and left-align thumbnail images that show your product, while right aligning the details of your sale or promotion.

A "blammie" is like a graphic sticker that overlays your image and highlights key text. It might be a circle, star, or rectangle shape with the words "Sale!" or "50% off!"

Embrace White Space

Don't try to fill every single inch of your image with text or graphic elements or "stuff." Let your graphics "breathe" with plenty of white space to create an image that feels clean and purposeful.

Stand out from the Crowd

While it's a good thing to sift through other Etsy shops and online stores, the last thing you want to do is look just like your competition. Once you've identified which style elements appeal to you in terms of colors and composition and feeling, hone in on what makes you unique—and highlight that visually. Let what makes you unique and interesting shine. Let it shape your images into a visual voice that's all yours. I can't tell you exactly how to do this—it takes some time—but you'll find it as you continue to work at articulating what you're trying to communicate and what makes you and your products special.

Read the Room

Appeal to YOUR customers: Don't try to appeal to everyone. In fact, if you try to make your images appealing to everyone, you'll find the approach counterproductive. What images and text speak to YOUR customers? (Hint: It might annoy or turn off people who are NOT your customers.) You don't need to sell your product to the world. You just need to sell it successfully to the people who are looking for your product and are aligned with the type of Etsy shop you want to create. If you're selling to nerds, embrace nerd lingo and images. If you're selling to moms, embrace mom talk. Find your demographic and speak to THEM.

Keep a 70/30 Ratio of Images to Text

Don't be tempted to overuse text. Images are what will catch your customer's eye for the most part. Use text as a secondary element, and use it sparingly (most of the time. If you deviate from this rule, go big with simple text and keep design elements minimal).

Match your Images to Your Text

Ask yourself, what is it I'm trying to communicate? What do I want my customer to feel when they see this graphic? Inspired? Comforted? Amused? Choose an image and text that both align with the message you want your customer to receive.

Be Intentional

Don't just include elements because they're cute, or a font because it's cool. Choose elements, fonts, and text because it complements your aesthetic, communicates key information to your customer, or showcases something about your product. Remember, the goal is for your customers not to be distracted by your design, but rather to entice them to take action or feel a certain way about your business.

Color is Important

While there aren't any hard and fast rules of color theory (because your culture, audience, and country will make a big difference in how your audience responds to different colors), you shouldn't choose colors randomly. Because people DO respond to color! Here's a few generalized principles of color theory that apply most of the time. Experiment, and dig in to figure out which colors your audience responds to best. Remember, seasonality and trends will play a role in which colors look best together. Keep your color palette fresh, and update it regularly.

- Red: Power, passion, speed. Commonly used to advertise food.

- Yellow: Your brain processes this color first, so it's an attention-grabber. Yellow communicates joy, happiness, and warmth.

- Orange: Playful, teasing, warm

- Gold: High end, expensive

- Silver: Refined, distinguished

- White: Clean, professional

- Pink: Sweet, feminine

- Green: Natural, fresh, cool

- Black: Strength, sophistication, elegant

- Blue: Calming, trustworthy

- Purple: Dignity, LGBTQIA+ ties

Contrast, Don't Clash

Without contrast, it's difficult to make elements of your images and graphics stand out. Take a look at the color wheel, and use colors that are opposite one another (e.g., red and green, yellow and purple, blue and orange). Contrast (including elements that are different from one another in shape, size, and texture) adds visual interest and keeps the eye moving across your image. However, using too many contrasting colors next to one another, in large amounts will create disorder and chaos to the eye (or clash).

Your goal will be to include enough contrasting colors elements in your images for visual interest, while using enough harmonious shapes, fonts, and color pairings (e.g., colors that are next to each other on the color wheel) for order and balance.

Elements of Successful Photos

In the last chapter, we talked about the different KINDS of photos you should include in a successful image. Now, let's dig a little deeper into what makes an individual photo appealing.

Thankfully, the elements of successful photos will include all the same elements of successful graphics that we covered above (e.g., contrasting elements, balance, color theory, alignment, standing out from the crowd) with a few key extras:

Models Matter

Who are you selling to? That audience needs to see themselves (or more accurately their aspirational selves, the people they WANT to be) in your photos. Choose models that appeal to your demographic (or whoever that demographic will be buying for) in terms of age, aesthetic, posture, styling, clothing, facial expressions, etc.

Setting Matters

Where you take your photos matters as much as who and what appears in them. Choose a setting that complements your models or product and appeals to your audience. A pristine, pinterest perfect house might look beautiful, but if you're selling counter-culture t-shirts, it's not the right environment. Your setting shouldn't distract from your product or your models, but rather enhance and support both. Remember, you need to look at the frame you'll be capturing when you determine what settings you'd like to use. A cool urban environment might be just the right setting, but if you need a lot of product close-ups, you might just get a lot of cement. Choose your setting with the types of photos you'll be taking in mind, and choose backgrounds that will complement your shot list.

Find that Perfect Lighting

This really can't be said enough: Filters and contrast settings can cover a multitude of minor sins in lighting, but they can't ever replace the beauty of really good, natural lighting. And they certainly can't correct bad lighting. Choose natural lighting whenever possible. The "golden hour" right before sunset is ideal and will give you that perfect diffused sunlight instead of harsh highlights and shadows. When shooting indoors, take the time (and invest the money as you are able) to create bright, beautifully lit photos indoors. Remember, photography is your Etsy shop's first impression. If the photos don't look beautiful, you'll sell far less than you could.

Pay for the Really Important Photos When Possible

Sometimes it's worth it to get your photography done professionally—particularly when you're after lifestyle photos with lots of moving parts (models, setting, lighting, vibe) or when you're after photos that will be highly visible (like your banner photos or main listing images). If budget is a concern (and of course it is, you're paving your own way here!), reach out to photography teachers at local Universities to connect with students who may want to build their portfolio.

Design Tools You Should Use and Master

Let me reassure you one more time: You don't need to be a graphic designer or photographer to succeed on Etsy. You just need to use the right tools. These are my favorites because they're easy to use, free or low cost, and they're confidence builders: even if you're new to design, you can create beautiful images using them.

Canva

Canva is the #1 tool I would recommend for non-designers. Why? Because it's a huge collection of very user-friendly, pre-designed templates, images, fonts, and layouts for you to access. Best of all? The free version has everything you need to succeed. The paid version (about $12/month) is worth it to me (you get access to even more features, like additional illustrations and the ability to download images with a transparent background).

I consider myself an intermediately skilled designer, and I plan to use Canva for the foreseeable future. If you have zero skills in design, you can search through templates until you find something you like, then swap out text and images. As you gain more skills and an eye for design, you can start to play with creating your own images. You'll find templates for Instagram, Facebook, banners, letterhead, business cards, you name it: It's on Canva.

Freelance Photographers

I already talked a bit about this earlier, but it's worth mentioning again. Freelance photographers are absolutely worth it for the crucial photography for your business. Learning the skills required to take a truly beautiful photo is hard, and it's worth your time to outsource this skill selectively to get that professional, beautiful touch to your business.

Photoshop and Lightroom (Adobe)

If you do delve into learning how to take your own photos, you should really subscribe to Photoshop and Lightroom (there's also Open Source software that's free and mimics these programs, but I prefer the real thing for usability. (You can get Photoshop and Lightroom for around $10 a month).

While Canva is wonderful, it'll only take you so far in being able to adjust and manipulate images and fonts (e.g., you can't create an arched font in Canva). These two programs are also great for your resume if you ever decide you want to branch out to a new career path. I taught myself how to use both of these programs. And it took a while. But I went a step at a time, focusing on specific tasks I needed to learn and gradually becoming familiar with how to use different tools and features to make my photos and *mockups look good.

When I talk about "mockups," I'm referring to images of full-sized product models that you can purchase and use in place of your own product photos.

Placeit.com

If you sell T-shirts, sweatshirts, leggings, iPhone cases, pillows, greeting cards (basically anything that you can loosely classify as "merch"), you'll find an entire database of models and staged mockups on Placeit.com. If you don't want to spend much on models or your own photography, Placeit allows you to create convincing mockups by uploading a .png (with a transparent background) that looks like it's been printed on the T-shirt/sweatshirt/leggings/iPhone case in the image.

Placeit continues to aggressively expand, adding more diverse models, some really pretty staged mockups, and even videos to showcase your products. It's super easy to use, and for less than $20 bucks you can download as many images as you want a month (and if you ever stop using the service, your images are still stored in your account).

Other Etsy Sellers

Other Etsy sellers are a WEALTH of resources for mockup photos, design help, and artwork elements. Just search for what you're seeking and see what comes up. For instance, for a long time I had no idea there were Etsy sellers who created beautiful flat-lay mockups of the exact blank tees I used—for a price that was way less than what I'd pay in time and energy and resources to take the photos myself.

Stuff We Learned the Hard Way about Design

I'm not a graphic designer by trade. I hadn't heard of Canva before I started my business, and I had never touched Photoshop. To be honest, I was really intimidated by the whole thing, and my first efforts were fledgling to say the least. So I guess it's fair to say that I learned everything the hard way!

Here are my biggest mistakes:

Getting too complicated: A lot of my initial efforts were full of too much text, too many fonts, and were just generally a little confusing. They weren't very successful, and it makes sense why.

Trying to do my own photography: I've learned that this is just one area of my business that I want to outsource, especially when it comes to the highly visible and important stuff. I've spent some time learning how to use Photoshop to edit my own photos that appear within listings, etc. But for those main images and for my model shots, I tap my favorite freelancer. It saves me so much time, stress, and energy.

Using blurry images without realizing it: It's really important to follow Etsy's sizing guidelines. Otherwise (especially if you're doing a million things at once), it's easy to think a photo looks good —without considering what that photo will look like when a customer zooms in. (And sees a blurry mess. TURNOFF.) I uploaded images that were too small and too low resolution far too often before I realized what I was doing in the early days.

Jumbled/clashing aesthetic: As my business started to actually take off, I failed to pay attention to the overall aesthetic of my shop. It ended up looking really disjointed with a lot of different types of photos and styles. That didn't necessarily hurt me when buyers viewed individual listings, but it did hurt my credibility as a business and wasn't exactly impressive to buyers who took a big-picture look at my shop as a whole.

I hope you're feeling more confident about graphics and design. You've got this. With some practice, an understanding of the fundamentals of good design, and what you just learned from my mistakes, get out there and take some pictures.

CHAPTER 5

How to Price Your Stuff

One of the top questions Etsy sellers (new and experienced alike) have is, "How should I price my products?" It's a good question, and it plays a pretty important role in your sales. Many sellers automatically assume that the answer is "as low as possible"; however, that's one of the biggest misconceptions about pricing. In fact, a race-to-the-bottom pricing approach can actually HURT your sales.

In this chapter, we're going to give you a solid foundation for how to price your products. And to do this well, it helps to understand how Etsy is positioned in the global ecommerce marketplace.

First, a Little Context

As a platform, Etsy is growing. It's becoming quite well-known and supports sellers across the globe. Etsy's performance is similar to the other large online sellers like Amazon and Walmart, Overstock.com and Wish. And because of this, far too many sellers try to compete in price with similar products outside the Etsy universe.

BUT, and this is vital: Etsy is not Walmart or Amazon (more on that in just a bit). Etsy has a reputation as a market of mom-and-pop shops selling handmade goods. And because of this reputation, customers go to Etsy looking for something they can't get on Amazon or Walmart—high-quality, handmade, unique items from sellers they can connect with in a personal way. And (this is the important part for pricing), *they'll pay for that.*

So, how exactly can you figure out the perfect price for your item? Let's get to it!

Do Your Research

To get your bearings, it's always a good idea to check out what other Etsy sellers are doing. This can at least give you an idea for the right price range to shoot for. But, as I said above, some sellers are selling themselves short or are selling cheaply made, mass produced products that really belong on Amazon and are often a turnoff to Etsy customers. So don't set a price as low or lower than the lowest you see. I promise, it won't work.

When you're looking for comparables, make sure the shop vibe and aesthetic line up with your own (or your aspirational vibe!) Choose four or five comparable shops that appear to have the same product quality, product type, and aesthetic. Create a price range based on those comparables.

A Formula for Success

Once you have that range determined, the next step is to determine your set costs (the costs you'll need to subtract from the price you charge your Etsy customers, a.k.a., your profit margin). Here's a basic formula for calculating how much you need to charge in order to make a profit.

- Calculate the cost of your materials and fixed expenses per item as accurately as possible (including Etsy fees, packaging, and shipping costs if you offer "free" shipping). We'll talk about Etsy's fee structures more in the next section.

- Add up any yearly shop expenses and divide by 12 to portion those expenses out monthly (e.g., any equipment or materials you purchase infrequently, yearly subscriptions, insurance costs).

- Add up all your average monthly expenses (e.g., rental space, utilities, and those portioned out yearly expenses) and divide those expenses by the average number of products you sell per month.

- Figure out exactly how much time you spend creating your item (labor) and pay yourself for your work (I usually estimate around 10-12 dollars an hour).

- Add everything up and multiply by 1.15 for wholesale (15% profit margin) or 1.30 for retail (30% profit margin). For newbies, wholesale is the price you offer for someone who wants to order in BULK then turn around and sell your products in their own venue. Retail is the price you'll charge to an end-consumer who is purchasing your product to enjoy themselves.

You'll generally offer your *wholesale price* only if someone wants to buy 50+ items. Your *retail price* should be the displayed price on your typical Etsy listing. Use this formula as a starting point, and compare it with the price range you calculated after looking at your #shopgoals competitors.

If your production costs mean that you would have to charge more than your competitors by a significant amount, it's time to look at your materials and sourcing. If your number is significantly lower, congratulations! You might have a high-margin item. Some products are very easy and cheap to produce, but people will pay significantly more than 30% markup. Don't be afraid to charge what the market will pay, if the situation allows.

Accounting for Etsy Fees and Ad Charges

To accurately determine your profit margins, you need to understand Etsy's fee structure for listings, transactions, and ads. Here's what you need to know:

Listing, Transaction, and Processing Fees

Like I mentioned earlier, you'll need to consider Etsy's fees when you determine your pricing because these fees apply to every sale you make.

Here's the breakdown of Etsy fees.

- Etsy charges $0.20 to post a listing for four months. (And if you offer a quantity of more than 1, you'll be charged $0.20 each time your product sells and your listing renews automatically.)

- When your item sells, Etsy charges a transaction fee, which is 6.5% of your sale price (including shipping costs). This fee increased from 5% to 6.5% as of April, 2022.

- Etsy also charges a payment processing fee when an item sells —3% + $0.25.

So, let's say you list a handmade coat for $100, shipping included. You'll be charged $0.20 when you list the item. When it sells, you'll be charged $6.50 in transaction fees, and $3.25 in processing fees. So, you need to account for $9.95 in Etsy fees for each $100 coat you sell.

Fees for Offsite Ads

In addition to these basic fees, small sellers have the option to participate in Etsy Offsite Ads, which comes with fees of its own (don't worry, we'll tell you ALL about offsite ads in Book 2 if you'd like to learn!). Sellers who make more than $10,000 a year in sales are actually automatically enrolled in this program (but it's not a bad thing, really).

But back to the fees. When a customer buys a product from an offsite ad, Etsy charges you 15% of the sale price. (Sellers making more than $10,000 a year are charged a discounted rate of 12% of the sale price for offsite ads.) So, if you're small and want to participate or if you have to participate like us, make sure to take these higher fees into account. These are sales you likely wouldn't make without the ad (Etsy is fronting the cost of advertising your item beyond Etsy's marketplace), so any profit you can glean from them is something to celebrate!

So, back to that $100 coat you sold. If the coat was sold as part of an offsite ad, you're out an additional $15. So, in total, your fees before shipping would weigh in at $23.45 even before you calculate for the cost of materials and shipping.

Fees for Native Etsy Ads

All sellers also have the option to participate in Native Etsy Ads. Somewhat confusingly, this program is different from Etsy Offsite Ads. Like the name implies, these ads are shown within the Etsy universe, instead of offsite on Google or other websites.

With Etsy Ads, there is no set percentage in fees. You decide how much you want to spend per day between $1 and $50 and Etsy will advertise your listings each day until your budget is gone. (If you're interested, we talk all about paid advertising options in Book 2). For our purposes here, just know that the fees for Native Etsy ads will depend on how heavily you want to utilize them.

Etsy Pricing Strategy: Don't Be Walmart/The Dollar Store

One of the most important parts of your Etsy pricing strategy (after you've accounted for all your fixed costs) is this: You are a handmade goddess/god. You are NOT Walmart. And you should price accordingly.

In other words, don't price your stuff too low. Now, Walmart and The Dollar Store definitely have their place in our culture, but there's really no place for cheaply made, disposable, mass-produced items on Etsy. Don't undercut yourself. Most sellers find that they make *more* sales if they up their prices a bit. For each product, there's a sweet spot, and once you find it, I guarantee your sales will jump considerably. Here's why:

Customers not only *don't mind* paying a little more on Etsy (than they would at Walmart or the Dollar Store), they actually *expect* to pay more, which means you can actually do your sales a lot of harm by pricing your items too low. Because if customers see you acting like Amazon or Walmart in terms of price, they'll often associate you with lower quality, mass-produced goods in a race to the bottom. Don't undersell yourself. Price your products with pride, while taking into account solid principles of pricing.

Finding the Pricing Sweet Spot Through Testing

Okay, so you've taken a good look at your fees, your production costs, and you've seen what your competition is doing. You feel the power of being a handmade creator running through your veins and you know you shouldn't undersell yourself. How do you find that exact pricing sweet spot, though?

There's always the "pick a number that feels right and see how the item sells over the next 30 days" method, which is what a lot of sellers do and what I did at first too. You can look at that list of comparables you made earlier and see where the TOP sellers are pricing their items and just go with that. This works pretty well for niche products, but less so for broad category items like earrings or abstract art, where pricing can be all over the place.

While both of the above methods will likely land you eventually on the right item price, you can get there faster by using Marmalead's price tool. Marmalead offers a free 14-day trial and then charges month-to-month ($19/month) after that and is worth it for the hours it'll save you, especially if you're just starting out.

When you type a keyword into Marmalead, it will give you the average price across Etsy of items ranking for that keyword. For example, Fourth Wave largely sells "feminist shirts," and Marmalead's price tool gives me a good idea of what the average "feminist shirt" is selling for on Etsy.

A/B testing within your shop is also a good way to test prices more quickly than the "guess and wait" method. Duplicate a listing (Etsy will allow you to copy a listing exactly) and list it twice, changing only the price and then watch both listings for 30 days to see which sells better. If the higher-priced listing is selling better, you can adjust both listings up and watch for another 30 days. This will help you hone in on the pricing sweet spot more quickly.

Warning! There are some downsides to duplicate listings. Customers may see both side-by-side in search results, which looks a little strange and can make customers see your shop as less professional. Also, if a customer does venture into your shop proper and sees a lot of the same listings over and over, they might be turned off by that as well. Once you start seeing views and sales for a listing, it's probably a good idea to get rid of any duplicates and focus on whichever (A or B) listing is performing better.

The Big Question: Should You Offer "Free" Shipping?

Etsy's big thing in 2019-2020 was offering free shipping site-wide. They really really want to compete with Amazon on this. And it's a little frustrating, because, as I've said before, Etsy is not Amazon or Walmart or the The Dollar Store. It's supposed to be more like a craft bazaar or an art fair. Nonetheless, Etsy is really encouraging sellers to offer free shipping, and they'll reward you for it not only with a boost in rank for listings with free shipping, but with a label across the bottom of your listing that says "free shipping" to entice buyers.

That said, Etsy's push for "free" shipping is rooted in sound psychology. Buyers are more likely to purchase a $30 product with "free shipping" than they are to purchase a $25.50 product with $4 shipping. Something about skipping that extra step, feeling like they got a freebie, and the simplicity of the price is enough to tip the scales.

So, here's what you do. Go ahead and offer free shipping to domestic customers, but raise your prices to cover the average shipping cost. For us, this meant pricing our shirts up about $3-4. It ended up being a good move—our number of sales didn't drop (or go up) despite the small price hike and we've had fewer abandoned carts.

Staying Competitive on Pricing as the Market Shifts

It's important to remember that Etsy is an ever-changing marketplace. Shifts in the economy, the job market, and other trends affect how likely someone is to buy on Etsy (and at what price). So your perfect pricing sweet spot won't stay the same forever. When I started Fourth Wave, there were approximately zero other shops selling feminist shirts on Etsy, and my products sold no matter how I priced them (within reason, of course). But as the market shifted, feminist and political shirts became much more common, which means I've needed to be more competitive in my pricing.

Regularly Pretend You're a Customer Visiting Your Shop

Etsy is constantly changing how it sorts and displays items to customers. I mention this because a little over a year ago, Etsy added a checkbox under the search criteria for "items under $25." I had been pricing my shirts at $25, so to qualify for this box, I set my shirt prices at $24.99, and, you guessed it, my sales jumped. With a click of a checkbox, a customer could eliminate a large portion of my competition, making it much more likely that person would find and purchase a shirt from my shop. So, it's a good idea to role-play a customer coming to your shop and see what options they have for weeding out competitors based on price.

Etsy adds new checkboxes all the time, to encourage buyers to hone in on the exact product and price range they want. Make sure you stay in the loop on these changes that can drastically affect your pricing strategy.

Estimating Shipping Costs

Shipping costs are going to differ depending on where your shipping *from* and *to*. I'm only going to talk about shipping from the US or Canada because Etsy has specific tools for both countries, so if you're not based in one of those two countries, this section may not help you much. You'll pretty much need to calculate your own shipping costs through whatever carrier you use in your country.

If you are a US or Canada based shop and want to know exactly how much it will cost to ship a single item, you can use Etsy's handy "Price Your Postage Tool."

It's a great tool for getting an idea about your shipping costs, but you don't want to have to use it for every item you ever ship. It's easier to estimate the average you'll be spending on shipping in future weeks or months in order to get a good idea for how much to budget for shipping. Here's what you need to know:

• Etsy gives sellers who ship through their platform a discounted rate (somewhere between 15%-30%), so **it's almost always cheaper to create your labels and ship through Etsy** rather than take everything to the post office.

• For USPS, package **shape will affect your shipping cost**. There are three categories: Letter, Flat, and Parcel. Etsy-calculated shipping pretty much assumes everything is a parcel, so if you sell cards, posters, or something like face masks that can be pressed flat inside a mailing envelope, you will need to use the custom shipping option or take stuff to the post office for accurate pricing. I've found that for cards and flat (squashable) items (like face masks), it's cheaper for me to use stamps rather than purchase labels through Etsy. Canada Post doesn't have a flat-parcel option, but if you sell cards or something similarly flat, definitely check out the pricing options for letters vs. parcels to decide how best to send your items.

- Etsy costs for parcels are largely dependent on weight, **approximately $0.30-$0.40 USD per ounce** (the price per ounce goes down as the item gets heavier). The heaviest package you can ship is 70 lbs through USPS and 30 kg through Canada Post. (If you sell really heavy stuff like furniture, I'll give some suggestions for cost-effective shipping below.)

- **Package size** can factor into the cost if your box or mailing tube is very large or unusual in shape. If your packaging is unusual (say, very long and thin or very large and flat), use the Price Your Postage Tool I mentioned above to get an idea of your shipping costs.

- **If you sell educational materials** from a shop in the US, you can take advantage of Media Mail prices.

Takeaway: For averaged-sized items, you can estimate your shipping costs at $0.30-$0.40 per ounce (under a pound is closer to $0.40/ounce and 3 lbs or more is closer to $0.30/ounce). These are better prices than you will get at the post office because Etsy shipping gives you a discount of "up to 30%" (again, larger items get closer to the full 30% while items under a pound get closer to 15% discount).

Shipping Really Large Items

Furniture is probably the most common example of the large items available on Etsy, and as you can imagine, shipping it can be daunting. Here are some tips if you ship furniture or something else too large to use Etsy's calculated shipping options:

- Keep in mind the type of customer that shops on Etsy. This person wants a very specific custom or hand-crafted piece, something they can't get at their local furniture store or on Amazon, and they're not only willing to pay more for it, they're happy to pay the hefty fees to have it shipped to them. In other words, if your shipping costs are in the $300's, don't freak out. Your customers will be okay with that.

- Get quotes from several carriers. Fast shipping carriers (FedEx, UPS, etc.) will generally charge more and slower carriers less. It's nice to offer customers options when you can: "Pay more to get the piece right away or less to receive it a few weeks out." For example, there are services like White Glove Shippers that offer shipping discounts but may only pick up items once a month for shipping, meaning money savings but shipping times of 5-6 weeks.

- Another tip is to use Etsy's option "fixed shipping costs" to enter an average price, but ask customers to message you for a precise shipping quote before they purchase. That way, you can adjust the cost based on where you're sending the item and charge the customer accordingly.

- Or offer free shipping, and adjust your price up $300 or so. You may want to wait until you've sold several pieces before trying out the free shipping option. The potential for losing money on shipping is a lot higher with very large items.

Stuff We Learned the Hard Way

Don't set your prices too low: Like many Etsy sellers, I priced my stuff WAY too low at first. I was so worried about turning off my potential customers that I didn't realize I was turning them off through the very way I hoped to win them.

When I finally raised my prices (and improved my shop aesthetic and keywords to match and inspire customer confidence that my prices were well-warranted), I saw my sales increase significantly.

Do the math: I also (like many Etsy sellers) have made the mistake of choosing pricing points on new products without doing my due diligence by looking at comparables first. It can be really tempting to choose a "gut-based" price, but if you choose wrong (and you probably will unless you are a genius), you'll send bad signals to Etsy's algorithms and your customers. Which means that your listing will earn negative points that aren't so easily erased even if you update your pricing strategy. Start things off on the right foot with your listings and price smart from the START.

CHAPTER 6

Customer Service

As an Etsy shop owner, you wear a LOT of hats. You are CEO, CMO, the design team, and the customer service team. If you don't approach this last role with the right mindset, it can cost you significantly and even slow your shop's growth. Here's what I mean:

You can have a truly amazing gem of a product, but if you treat your customers with a hit-or-miss bedside—or I guess *web-side*—manner, you're going to earn yourself bad reviews. And I won't sugarcoat this: Bad reviews will kill your business in the short and long-term.

Remember, part of the reason your buyers come to Etsy in the first place is to have a more personal, human experience and to support a smaller shop that feels more human than corporate. If you seem annoyed by messages, don't respond to people promptly, or craft automated messages that sound, well, automated, you're going to turn people off.

The bottom line? Good customer service equates to five-star reviews. And five-star reviews are a powerful signal to buyers that your shop can be trusted. They also raise your shop quality score significantly and help your listings rank higher in Etsy's algorithms.

Let's explore a few key best practices in customer service that will help you earn those sweet, sweet five-star reviews (and possibly a new Star Seller Badge).

Best Practices in Customer Service

These best-practices are the end result of my ten years of customer service experience in Etsy. The more closely I adhere to them, the more five-star reviews I get.

Promise with Precision, Over Deliver

You know that saying, "Under promise, over deliver?" I'm going to recommend a bit of an alternative: "Promise with precision, over deliver."

Promise with Precision

Your sales will suffer if you sandbag your product or include mediocre descriptions. You need sparkling, clean, beautiful, compelling images and text to catch a potential buyer's eye and encourage them to add your product to their shopping cart. Use your photos and listing descriptions to highlight every single amazing feature of your product, and don't hold back! But you need to be absolutely accurate in your descriptions and images. Don't use super-saturated photos that distort colors. Don't try to make something sound bigger, softer, brighter, etc. (you get the idea) than it is to make a sale. You'll only set your buyers up for disappointment, which will show in your reviews.

Do your handmade items vary somewhat from the listing photo, by nature of being handmade? Tell your buyers! Do you need a little longer to ship everything? Tell your buyers why, and create accurate shipping profiles.

Over Deliver

Okay, now for the fun part: Over deliver in ways your customer won't expect—so usually in some way that's related to but not directly involving the product you've sold. Surprise and delight your customer with something a little extra.

When our expectations are met, we feel pleased. When our expectations are met and we get a little surprise or thrill we weren't expecting, we feel delighted. Aim for giving your customers that feeling of delight in as many ways as you can without slowing down your process or adding a lot of extra expense. These are all ideas that have worked well for me, but I'd encourage you to combine your creativity with what you know about your target audience. Don't be afraid to play around a little bit and think outside the box.

- Use fun packaging that makes your customers smile. This packaging usually doesn't cost much more than the plain stuff, so why be plain? Some of my personal favorites are poly mailers with unicorns, donuts, or flamingos. (Check out Book 3 for more info on where you can cheaply and easily source packaging, notes, stickers, etc.)

- Include a handwritten note. It doesn't have to be long. It just has to be handwritten. I prefer writing these notes on stick-on kraft gift labels since I sell t-shirts. That way my note doesn't get lost in the packaging when it's opened.

- Buy custom bulk decals or bumper stickers that include a fun message your buyer will want to display (and include your company logo or name very unobtrusively in the corner).

- Add tags or labels to your product with a humorous or inspirational quote. You can also buy custom stamps to add a special touch to the outside of paper packaging.

- Create a lighthearted, fun purchase confirmation. Etsy allows you to customize the message that gets sent to buyers any time they make a purchase. Don't be shy about using humor and down-to-earth language in this message. For instance, here's what my purchase confirmation message says:

Please stand by as your order from Fourth Wave is infused with solidarity, a feminist fist bump, and, well, ink and stuff. I hope wearing it reminds you to "Let the beauty of what you love be what you do."

If you would, take a moment to double-check that you entered the correct shipping information, to avoid possible delays (Etsy's system can be a bit confusing!) Thank you again for your order!

Get 15% off when you sign up for our newsletter! Click here to subscribe: https://bit.ly/2LWYYEh

A bit of humor, a helpful reminder (that helps catch a surprising number of incorrect shipping addresses), and a plug for our newsletter that adds value.

- Use your shipping message as another way to thank your buyer for shopping with a small business (this feels good!), and tell them that you hope they love their product.

Notifications and Communication

In today's fast-paced, web-based world, people expect a response to electronic queries pretty promptly.

What does that mean? For a while, I kept my Etsy notifications set to alert me any time I received a message (or "Convo") from a buyer. But to be honest, that stressed me out, and I wasn't crafting the best replies because inevitably those convos came through while I was working on something else.

I've found that a more sustainable system is to set aside two different times per day when I will check my Etsy convos. I make sure I'm in a good headspace, I'm not hangry, and I'm not feeling particularly stressed out by anything. And then I check out my Etsy convos and respond to them all. I've never had anyone express irritation for slow responses; on the contrary, we've gotten lots of comments about prompt replies and helpful responses.

Make sure you check over weekends and holidays, but I usually decrease my response frequency to once per day. You don't want to burn yourself out or add too much stress. As your shop grows, consider adding a part-time freelance position that's just a few hours a week to help you respond to messages.

If you're on vacation and want to unplug (and you absolutely should do that!) You have the option to set an away message in Etsy. Make sure to be thoughtful (your buyer's questions are important, and if they aren't answered, you may lose a sale), and to reassure buyers that you are taking a bit of much-needed time away from your computer. Then let them know exactly when they can expect a response (and follow through!).

You can also choose to provide an "emergency" email where you can be reached if someone simply must talk to you. Most people won't use it, but the ones who do are the same ones who will leave you a poor review for not responding to them—so bite the bullet and respond!

Don't Make It Personal

This sounds easy but is actually really hard. On Etsy more than any other platform or marketplace, you ARE your product. As a handmade item, it's an extension of you. If a customer sends a message complaining about quality, the fact that it didn't ship with Amazon-Prime warp speed, or simply doesn't appreciate it as much as you think they should, it's all too easy to respond with a defensive, curt, or snarky reply.

The brief satisfaction of sending back the perfect zinger will be short lived. Most people who complain are looking for validation and want your help solving a problem. They're not out to hurt your feelings or your shop's success (even though it may feel like it at the time.) Respond with compassion, validate their feelings, and make it all about them (not you). How you choose to respond will depend on your product and the particular complaint, but it's my policy to do whatever it takes within reason to create a happy customer and a great review. Those good reviews are worth far more to me than a partial loss I'll take by sending a replacement, allowing an exchange (even if it's not allowed in my policies) or sympathizing with someone who didn't get their product immediately.

Outsource If You Can

I'll say it again: It's really freaking hard not to take things personally sometimes. As my shop got bigger, I felt burnt out by dealing with customer questions and complaints. There were relatively few (maybe a couple out of every hundred orders I sent out), but most of the time you don't hear from the happy folks (except in your glowing reviews, read those often!) but rather the folks with a bone to pick.

I decided to outsource my customer service to a freelancer who would spend just a couple hours a week answering my questions and dealing with customer issues. It was one of the best things I've ever done for my shop. Not only is Leesa cheerful, helpful, and my customers love her (after all, it's not personal to her when someone doesn't cherish my hard work), but she has a background in hospitality and is incredibly good at making my customers feel heard and appreciated.

If you work with a partner, take turns doing customer service if you can to give each other a breather and enjoy tapping out of the constant stream of questions and comments for periods of time.

Take the Loss and Assume the Best

As much as you're in the business of creating t-shirts, artisan jams, princess dresses, or decals, you're in the business of making your customers happy. Your shop can't succeed without them. Any one negative review your shop receives hurts you more than any one positive review helps.

So what does that mean? Take the loss. Especially if it was your fault anyway (in the customer's mind, not yours). If your customer feels unhappy, your response should proportionally reflect the feelings they're projecting at you—no matter how justified or not you feel they are. Their reality is their reality, and to succeed you'll need to meet them where they're at. Take the loss to keep a happy customer. This doesn't have to mean a total loss, but it usually means giving up something extra for the long-term goal of your success. Taking the loss for the greater good looks like this in my shop, depending on the particular complaint or the customer's demeanor (I don't do all of these every time a customer complains—I pick the one that I think will best satisfy the unhappy customer):

- Sending out a new product completely free of charge.

- Offering a special discount for future orders.

- Including a unique goodie or note in an order (for example, if the order hasn't arrived on the customer's timeline).

- Offering to cancel the order and refund the customer (if I think the customer won't be happy no matter what I do and is likely to leave a bad review no matter what).

- Authorizing a return even if the customer has washed their item or kept it longer than 14 days (my policy).

- Sending out a replacement for an item that was lost in the mail (not my fault, but I earn a happy customer).

Do I get taken advantage of now and then? Probably. But the number of customers who complain is low enough, and I'm committed to their happiness enough that it isn't a big deal in the scheme of things.

Assuming good intentions and taking the loss instead of adopting an attitude of suspicion has been key to my success.

Replacements, Refunds, and Lost Packages

I see questions about these three issues on the Etsy forums all the time. "What should I do if the post office loses my customer's package? It's not my fault!" Or "This customer is asking for a replacement when it's against my shop policy. What should I do?"

Here's the thing: Etsy will stand behind you if you have clearly stated shop policies and decide to hold your ground. Etsy will also stand behind you refusing to refund or replace an order that got lost in the mail (as long as it was shipped with an Etsy label and tracking shows it's in the system). Does that mean you should hold your ground and be a hard-nose? As you can probably guess from my previous sections, I wouldn't recommend it in most cases.

In most cases, swallow your annoyance and keep the big picture in mind. Be generous, be flexible, and strive for great reviews. Unless this happens to you all the time (and if it does, there's likely a reason for it/some work you need to do on your product or descriptions), do the thing that will make your customer happy, even if your policies or Etsy's policies will support you in not doing so.

That's not an absolute rule. Sometimes (RARELY) your instincts tell you that a customer is just yanking your chain. They'll take the free product and give you a bad review to boot. Or they don't bother reaching out to you and hit you with a terrible review. What should you do in that case? Read on:

Dealing with Bad Reviews

So what happens when you've been as pleasant as a peach and still get some furious person who leaves you a steaming, stinking one- or two- or three-star review?

First things first: Deep breath. Bad reviews suck. They suck so much. It feels terrible to see your hard work disparaged, especially for silly reasons (and you WILL see some silly reasons. I once got a one-star review from a woman who "Loved her shirt, but did this ship by COVERED WAGON?" (The shirt shipped in five business days, as stated in my shipping timeframes and product descriptions since it is handmade).

There's a few important strategies for dealing with bad reviews. Start with number one, and proceed from there.

1. You took that deep breath, right? Remind yourself that bad reviews happen, all shops get them, and it doesn't mean you're a terrible person or artist. People are complicated. If I'm sure I'm doing my best, I imagine to myself that this person may have hemorrhoids flaring up.

2. Reach out, kindly, through Etsy messaging. After you've taken that deep breath. Something along the lines of, "Hey Karen, I just saw your review. I wanted to let you know I'm so sorry you were disappointed in your shirt. It sounds like you were expecting it for a birthday and it didn't arrive in time. I'd feel disappointed if I were in your shoes too. I was wondering if I could offer you a partial discount on your order to make it up to you? I appreciate your order so much. I'm so proud of my work, and I want you to love it too. As a small business, I will never take my customers for granted."

3. Make the message your own. Don't justify yourself. Don't rationalize what happened (unless there is a HUGE piece of information they are missing), and don't ask them to change their review. Just empathize and offer your best way to fix it. You'd be shocked at how many people will respond with gratitude and change their review without being asked. For the ones that respond with gratitude (but haven't changed their review after a few days), try sending another message like this:
    "Hey Karen, I just wanted to reach out to you to ask if there's anything you'd like to change in your public review before I

reply to it. I know how frustrated you were when you wrote it (completely understandable). If you're set on the review, I respect that, but I try to follow up with my customers first to make sure they'd like to keep the review as is first before I reply to the review as a shop owner (since my response will lock the review and prevent future edits for both of us)! Hope you are doing well."

Most of the time, you'll get a bump in stars (the buyer can edit their review any time until you respond to the review publicly).

4.   If you don't hear back from the customer, they aren't willing to work with you, or your gut feeling tells you that this is one of those situations where someone is just mad and taking it out on you (this is rare but happens), go ahead and respond publicly. To respond publicly to a review, find the customer in your orders tab in the Etsy dashboard. You'll see the review attached to that customer's order. Click on the star rating, and then type your response in the dialogue box that appears. Stick to the facts, stay professional, and take the high road. Other potential buyers will read your response for more information, and they may choose to purchase (or not) based on your reasonable response. Don't be afraid to add additional context or refute details that the (angry) person included in their review, but don't come across as spiteful or mean. Once you reply in this dialogue box, it locks the review. The customer can't respond or edit their original review (and you won't be able to edit your response, either so make sure you're happy with your response).

5.   Respond to bad reviews quickly and make it a practice of checking for them regularly. The sooner you reply, the more likely you are to get a positive resolution.

Encouraging Five-Star Reviews

Isn't that what we've been talking about this WHOLE time? Sort of. Being a relatable, awesome shop owner with great boundaries who avoids bad-review pitfalls will earn you some organic good reviews. But here's a surprisingly simple trick many Etsy shop owners overlook: To get the most good reviews, you have to ask for them. According to BrightLocal's article "Local Customer Review Survey," a whopping 70% of customers will leave you a review if you simply ASK. And since 97% of buyers look at reviews extensively before making a purchase, gathering all the positive reviews you can is really, really important.

Everybody's busy. And Etsy tries to help out with that fact by giving your buyers a notification when they log into their Etsy account, right at the top of their screen, that shows recent purchases and asks them to rate those purchases. Easy, peasy.

Unfortunately, many buyers will still ignore that notification. What encourages them to take the extra 10 seconds to give you a good review? You ask.

Send your ask in the text of your automated shipping notification and your order confirmation. In both places, thank your buyer for their purchase. Tell your buyer that as a small-business owner and handmade artist, you appreciate each and every one of your customers and that a five-star review would mean the world to you. You hope they love their purchase, and encourage them to reach out to you with any questions!

If you've successfully associated your shop and this purchase with a human, positive message that makes your customer feel like an important part of your shop (and I daresay life), that memory is likely to ping in their mind when they see the notification pop up on their Etsy dashboard, asking them to rate their purchase. It's such a simple way to encourage your buyers to take the extra ten seconds to review you.

Setting Boundaries

The customer is always right. Which means you should strive to make customers happy even if it means setting yourself on fire, right?

No. Don't do that. You'll set yourself up for burnout and a bad experience. And you won't have better reviews or sales to show for it. Instead, you'll be spending a lot of time on one or two orders, while you could have been doing A, B, or C to make the majority of your customers happier.

What do boundaries look like? It'll vary depending on your shop, your personality, and your products. Here's what boundaries look like for me:

- I create clear shop policies that address the most common questions my customers may have or scenarios that tend to crop up (for example, lost packages, returns, exchanges, etc.) The stuff that's inevitably going to happen. Your customers may not read all of your policies, but most reasonable customers will recognize that they had the option to read those policies before making a purchase (and will be easier to deal with when you need to hold to your boundaries because of it).

- Keeping my shipping timeframes up to date, especially around the holidays. Again, your customers may not read them, but they are easily visible and help create boundaries for your shop.

- I don't offer rush shipping. For me, rush shipping means an extra drive to my studio, gambling whether the post office will get the package there on time (it often doesn't when you really need it to, Murphy's law), and lots of time with back-and-forth. If a customer asks me about rush shipping, I explain that "Due to the handmade nature of my products, I'm not able to offer rush shipping." Sometimes this is hard to do when someone is oh so sweet and has a birthday the next day, or whatever. But remember: Someone's poor planning is NOT your emergency. Be polite, and keep your boundaries (which you've backed up with your shipping timeframes and shop policies, right?)

- For any custom orders I offer, I lay out very specifically in the listing description what IS and is NOT included. For example, I offer custom family reunion t-shirts. If the customer provides an image (EXACTLY as they want it, in 300 DPI, correctly sized) there is no artwork fee. If I have to design something, I charge an art prep fee and require specific details. This keeps me from doing free work.

- I don't send free samples. Hardly ever, anyway. And I rarely send out free stuff to influencers. Why? Because half the time it works out, and half the time you never hear from them again. And those aren't good odds. HOWEVER, I do often donate items to good causes that align with my business. Silent auctions, gift baskets that include my products, or even sponsorship of good causes with high visibility can be a great feel-good opportunity that also puts your business in front of new customers (make sure you attach tags to your products that you send out into the world and include business cards!)

- I encourage communication through Etsy. In the event that something goes haywire, I have a record of all convos right in Etsy's app.

Bottom line: Be human in your customer service. But be a confident, kind human with boundaries that keep you sane and your customers happy.

A Few Thoughts About the Star Seller Program

In September of 2021, Etsy rolled out its Star Seller Program as "a way to recognize and reward Etsy sellers who consistently provide an excellent customer experience."

The Basics of the Star Seller Program

Here's the basics of what you need to know. Keep in mind that (in part because of a somewhat poor experience for many sellers), this program is still evolving. But for now:

To even be in the running for the Star Seller badge:

- Your shop has to be on Etsy for at least 90 days

- Your shop must have 10 orders OR made at least $300 during that time.

Each month, the Star Seller Program "grades" Etsy shops based on three metrics:

- Message response times (95% of your messages got a reply in under 24 hours)

- Five-star ratings (at least 95% of your reviews must be five-stars)

- 95% on-time shipping WITH tracking (E.g., did your orders ship out within the timeframe you specified in your shipping settings for that particular product and did you include tracking?). Note: This is another good reason to use Etsy labels!

- The "grades" Etsy assigns are based on performance in these three areas over the previous 90 days, and shops that score 95% or above in all three metrics get the Star Seller badge.

Why Did Etsy Roll Out the Star Seller Program?

Etsy has become increasingly popular over the last few years. As of 2021, there were over 5 million sellers on the platform, and that number continues to grow.

Etsy obviously wants customers to have a good experience on its platform. The powers that be created the Star Seller Program both as a way to motivate good customer service and to let customers know when a product they're eyeing is being sold by an exceptionally high-performing shop.

Frequently Asked Questions About the Star Seller Program

The new program begs a lot of questions (we certainly scoured the resources available for these answers as soon as possible!). Here's the top questions and answers about the program:

Does the Star Seller Program Affect My Placement in Search?

This is a big question. And for now, the answer is no: Shops that qualify for the Star Seller badge *don't* currently get a boost in ranking. Conversely, shops that *don't* qualify won't have their listings demoted in ranking.

How Does Star Seller Benefit Me?

There are some benefits for sellers who achieve Star Seller status. Notably: All of the seller's listings will display a small purple star badge stating that that product is being sold by a Star Seller shop. And Etsy's system DOES give preference to Star Sellers when displaying suggested listings to buyers and when showing featured listings on the Etsy homepage.

How Attainable Is the Star Seller Badge?

The answer to this question depends a lot on your shop type. If you sell very straightforward items (e.g. coffee mugs) and have clockwork shipping and customer service, it may be possible to consistently earn the Star Seller badge.

However, for an Etsy shop like ours (that has a lot of variables at play with sizing and color), it can sometimes be more difficult to predict customers' responses. (For example, if the color of the shirt wasn't QUITE what someone expected because of their monitor display, or the size wasn't what they'd anticipated based on ordering from a different Etsy shop, they might choose to leave a 4-star review).

Basically, for many Etsy shops the Star Seller badge is a bit of a slippery thing: You can get it one month and it'll be gone the next. Because Etsy assesses each shop every month for how they performed over the previous 90 days, your Star Seller badge may not last very long.

How Is the Program Likely to Evolve?

There are some sticky points for the program, and it clearly still needs some honing. In other words, what Etsy thinks it's measuring isn't always exactly reflective of what's going on in reality. Here's what we mean:

Message Response Rate: Thankfully, Etsy has done some serious honing in this category since the Star Seller program launched. Etsy started out expecting sellers to answer EVERY message AND be the one to have the last word every time. They got some feedback about that from a lot of extremely frustrated sellers and made some changes. Now, sellers must respond within 24 hours to the *first message* in a conversation. None of your other responses count for or against you! Also, you don't have to respond to messages from Etsy itself. As for spam messages, you don't need to respond to them, but you DO need to mark them as spam.

Five-Star Ratings: This is exactly what it sounds like (unfortunately). Sellers basically get one point for each five-star rating they receive and zero points for ratings of four-stars and below. Etsy then divides the number of five-star ratings by the total number of ratings received and turns that into a percentage. This appears to be the metric that causes the most sellers to miss out on the Star Seller badge. And it's definitely the one that sellers have the least control over because a "good" rating can mean different things to different customers, and Etsy's decision to count a four-star rating with the same weight as a one-star rating is quite obviously not representative of which shops have good customer service and which don't.

Shipping: To meet the shipping requirement, sellers must include tracking information for 95% of their orders. For US sellers, this means 95% of ALL orders. You can mark orders that are picked up by the customer as finished without including shipping information, but this will count against your Star Selling shipping "grade." Hopefully, Etsy figures out some way to reconcile this in the future. For some countries that don't provide affordable tracking, Etsy only asks for tracking for items over a certain amount (equivalent to about $15 USD in whatever currency the seller uses).

The Cliff's Notes on the Star Seller Program

Don't sweat the Star Seller Badge too much. If you don't qualify for the badge or are unlikely to be able to qualify, don't spend too much time and energy trying. Etsy has introduced a number of programs meant to incentivize sellers over the years, and this is just the latest iteration.

For now, the program isn't affecting ranking. This means that you're still better off honing your niche and keywords and doing some marketing and advertising to get eyeballs on your products than you are spending all your time trying to achieve Star Seller status. Do what you can: Respond to convos, provide the best customer service possible, and include tracking information for shipments as often as possible. But remember that the Star Seller program is far from perfect, and if you're doing the best you can and running an incredible shop, that will show in your performance.

Dealing with Claims against Your Shop

Claims are a different beast than bad reviews. Claims are private—between you and the buyer, and they happen if a buyer believes you have been dishonest in your descriptions or somehow cheated them out of their money. If the buyer contacts you with a problem, and you don't resolve it within 3 days, the buyer can escalate the issue to Etsy.

Etsy is NOT motivated to deal with squabbles. Even after someone has opened a case, Etsy requires the buyer and seller to try to figure it out for an additional three days before they intervene. (Unless the situation is super serious or there's harassment and potential scary stuff involved, then they may intervene earlier.) They'll give the buyer and seller every opportunity to deal with this issue among themselves and will really only step in if the buyer is quite persistent and insists the issue can't be resolved without help. For issues of package non-delivery, the claim will automatically be closed if you used an Etsy shipping label and the package is confirmed delivered via tracking.

Buyers have 100 days to open a claim from the time they receive their item. If you have a claim brought against your shop, and you're gridlocked with a customer, Etsy will step in and mediate. If you are in the wrong, Etsy can garnish your shop payment account to refund the customer. If you aren't willing to participate in mediation or are unhelpful, Etsy can even suspend your account. So be helpful and available if a claim is brought against you.

The good news? In the 10 years I've been an Etsy shop owner, I've had two claims brought against my shop. Both for packages that never showed up, and the buyers filed the claims without even reaching out to me. Claims are rare. You might deal with them, but if you're doing other stuff right in customer service, it should be very, very infrequently.

Stuff We Learned the Hard Way

I've learned a lot of things the hard way about customer service over the years. Every single piece of advice I've shared here represents something I've done wrong—and learned better from—at one point or another over the years. I've bent over backwards when I shouldn't have, stretched my boundaries until I felt used and undervalued, responded to customers in the heat of the moment and earned a bad review, and failed to ASK my customers for reviews for WAY, way too long.

Learn from my mistakes, and start earning those five-star reviews.

CHAPTER 7

Troubleshooting Your Etsy Account

At this point, I hope that you're up to your elbows in the business of creating a solid foundation for your Etsy shop. I hope you're creating a plan to hone the key components of your shop that will speak directly to Etsy's algorithm. I hope you're honing your listing titles and descriptions. I hope you're mining keywords like crazy and keeping track of your success (and then doing more of it). I hope you're experimenting with the easy-to-use tools in design and photography that will give you an edge over your competition.

And if you're doing those things, you may run into technical trouble. It happens to the best of us. Sometimes it's Etsy's fault, sometimes it's the internet's fault, and sometimes it's just a knowledge gap.

In this chapter, we wanted to give you a few tools for troubleshooting some of the most common questions and issues you might run across as you build your Etsy empire. We obviously can't imagine every single situation out there, but we can give you solid tools for solving these questions and issues as they arise. SO, let's get troubleshooting.

HELP! What to Do When Things Go Sideways

Sometimes, stuff goes wrong, especially when selling online (the internet is an ever changing beast). One of your Etsy listings may get wrongfully taken down. Something may go wrong during a payment or while you're trying to create and print shipping labels. An internet glitch or an Etsy bug may prevent you from uploading images or saving a listing you've worked really hard on (so frustrating!). And sometimes, you just want ideas for how to improve your shop. There are a number of routes you can take to find resolutions, and the first is always to check the Etsy Forums.

Finding Answers with the Etsy Community Forums

The Etsy community forums are located at community.etsy.com. This is where Etsy itself puts announcements about updates, opportunities, and new features for Etsy sellers. And it's also where sellers can post questions and contribute to discussions.

If something is wonky on the Etsy site, you can take comfort (and get actual solutions) from other Etsy sellers and Etsy's staff on these forums.

It's helpful to know that Etsy's staff monitors these discussions fairly closely and contributes when questions can't be answered by other sellers. It's also a good idea to contribute when you can to these forums, especially as you become a more experienced seller, because you'll want to keep them active in case you have a question in the future.

Help! There's a Bug or Tech Issue

One of the most frustrating situations is a bug or a glitch in Etsy's website. You try to upload a listing and get an "uh oh" message no matter what you do. That's the kind of side-quest nobody wants to spend time on. So, what can you do?

Figuring Out Where the Problem is Occurring

When trying to resolve a problem with your Etsy shop, figuring out whose fault the problem is more than half the battle. I realize that it sounds really petty when I put it like that, but placing blame in these situations is less about relieving yourself of responsibility than discovering who you need to contact (if anyone) to get the problem fixed.

Just like all online platforms, Etsy is constantly revising and updating its site, search algorithm, and features, and more often than is convenient, things go wrong. Are you suddenly having trouble uploading photos to a listing? Or updating your About Section when you've never had a problem with it before? Check the forums. If other sellers are having the same problems at the same time, it's probably Etsy's fault, and if the problem is big enough, they're probably working feverishly to fix it.

Another culprit for sudden and random technical issues may be your internet browser. Is your browser blocking pop-ups? Turn that blocker off for Etsy's domain. Etsy also doesn't really work for sellers using Firefox. Etsy's front-end site works there, so customers can browse Etsy and make purchases, but the backend, where sellers do their thing, isn't optimized for Firefox, which means getting a listing up is really painful. You're much better off using Google Chrome (best), Microsoft's Internet Explorer, or Apple's Safari when making changes within your Etsy's shop.

If you're using the Sell on Etsy app on your phone, it's good to know that the app is really buggy on Android phones (Google and Samsung) and works much better on iPhone. By all means, use the app on your Android phone, but recognize that some features won't work, and you'll need to perform certain actions on your computer instead.

Contacting Etsy about Bugs and Issues on Their Platform

Every once in a while, you'll encounter a problem with Etsy's platform that you can't resolve, and you'll need to contact Etsy's support team. To do this, go to help.etsy.com. You'll need to log in to your Etsy account if you're not already. This website puts you through your paces before allowing you to contact a real human. Etsy really wants you to make sure you can't resolve your issue by reading through the forums, Etsy's FAQ, or any of their other literature. If you're seeing what you think may be a bug, make sure to check Etsy's "Known Issues" at the very bottom of the help page under the section "Your Etsy Account." Etsy's staff lists here the problems sellers have brought to their attention that they're working on but haven't yet fixed.

If you still have questions or need to send feedback after scouring Etsy's help page, first click on the subject related to the type of problem you're having, scroll to the bottom of that page and click the black button that says "Contact Support." Just so you don't go looking for it, I want to emphasize that this button doesn't exist until you click the link related to your specific problem.

Even this button will take you to a list of issues, from which you need to further select the problem you're experiencing. Keep selecting stuff even if the options don't quite describe your problem. A few clicks deep, you'll finally be able to send a message through the browser to Etsy's customer service support desk, and they'll email you back within a day or so.

Help! Someone Copied My Work

Sometimes you'll find trouble when you run into a bug on the Etsy site or need help figuring out a technical question. And sometimes trouble comes knocking on your door when somebody yoinks your product and creates a copycat.

This can be one of the most upsetting situations to deal with, but unfortunately it's pretty common. But the good news is you have options, and Etsy has your back.

Here's the deal: Your original creations are considered under copyright the moment you publish them in your Etsy shop. You can indicate this by placing a little © (copyright sign) next to the name of your item in the listing description, but you don't have to—that © is more of a reminder to others that stealing your work is against the law. Copyright protection makes the most sense for designs, art, and handmade items that are unique and couldn't be created by someone else without the other seller having seen your item and deliberately copying it. Basically, the more unique your product is, the stronger the copyright protection.

Copyright law is complicated, and even if you have that little © next to the name of your product, it's not always easy to know what to do when someone copies your idea. So here's what you do:

Dealing with Copyright Infringement

What should you do if you think someone has copied your work? There are several actions you can take depending on where you find the copy and how receptive you believe the copycat will be.

One factor to consider in the discussion about copyrights is how obvious the copy actually is. Did another seller create a product similar to yours? Or is the product exactly the same? Is that person using your images, title, or listing description to sell the product in their store? I have the most trouble with this in Fourth Wave because people copy and sell my t-shirt designs as SVGs, which they then sell to other t-shirt makers. Sometimes my copyrighted designs turn up all over the internet, often sold by people who paid for the design and believed it was sold to them legally. It's important to note that even if someone purchased a copyrighted SVG in good faith, they still need to honor your copyright and take the image down, since the image was sold illegally.

If you can't get a hold of a seller or they refuse to honor your copyright, you can file an Intellectual Property Infringement Report within Etsy, and Etsy Legal will deactivate the offending listing after they have reviewed your claim. The other seller has the option to file a Counter Notice if they think your report is incorrect. Most true copycats won't do this though because they know exactly what they're doing in copying your work.

If you discover your product has been copied and is being sold by a seller on a platform outside Etsy, you should again begin by contacting the seller. If that doesn't work, you can go over a seller's head, to the platform (e.g. eBay, Amazon) or the web host (Shopify, Squarespace, Blogger) by sending a DMCA (Digital Millennium

Copyright Act) takedown letter (for US-based platforms). The DMCA is an anti-piracy act protecting digital content and online items that legally requires a web hosting service to take down listings on their platform that violate copyright.

All of the large US-based platforms have a letter you can fill out, sign, and send, and there are generic "notices of infringement" you can modify and send to smaller platforms like the blog IPWatchdog.

Most other countries have similar copyright protection laws that you can point to for backup when demanding a take down if the copycat is selling on a non-US platform—"Notice and Notice" in Canada and the EUCD in Europe.

Help! I Have a Great Product, but I'm Not Getting Any Sales

I know that a lot of the last section was pretty technical with a pinch of legalese sprinkled in. Now, it's time to talk about some of the more common issues you may run into as an Etsy seller.

What happens when you've just launched your Etsy store or have had it up for a few months, but you're not getting many (or any) sales? Frustration and discouragement, and sometimes a feeling of personal betrayal. Are you doing something wrong? Doesn't anyone want the products you made with such love and care? What is *going on*?

Stage 1 Self Shop Audit: Product and Shop Quality

Before you throw the baby out with the bathwater, perform a quick audit of your Etsy shop by checking the following things.

Have you done your due diligence in making sure you have a healthy Etsy shop (e.g., the information in the previous six chapters)? Specifically your keywords and listings, the heart of your Etsy shop? If you rushed through setup and threw some listings together without doing much research or work on the backend, it's time to spend some serious hours getting your shop in shape.

Do you have a winning product? Are there other sellers on Etsy selling what you sell? Type the name of your product into the Etsy search bar and see how many shops come up. Click on one of these shops—does it have any sales? (The number of sales is listed under the Shop Name.) Scroll down—does the shop have any reviews? Are they good reviews? If other people are selling similar products to yours with good success, chances are that you have missed (or rushed through) some of the steps required to lay a solid foundation for your shop.

If there really aren't any other shops selling what you sell or the shops selling these items have very few sales and reviews, there may simply be no market (at least on Etsy) for what you're selling. Your product may sell better in person at a craft bazaar or in a boutique, or on another platform like Amazon or a quirky online shop with a very tight niche. Or, maybe, it's time to try selling something else entirely.

Again, if you find that similar products are indeed selling well in other Etsy shops, you'll need to take a hard look at your listings and your shop. You may even want to ask someone else (a friend or family member who can be honest with you) to take a look at your shop and give feedback. Consider these questions in particular: (1) Are your thumbnail images high quality and eye-catching? (2) Do your titles and descriptions describe what you're selling? (3) Is your shop professional looking and consistent in theme and tone? (4) Are you using all 13 tags?

If you find your shop lacking in some or all of these key elements, you've likely identified the reason for your lack of sales. Carefully read (and implement) Chapter 1 on Etsy shops and Chapter 2 on listings, and employ the tips and tricks there. Low-quality images, haphazard organization and design, and incomplete listings are some of the most common causes for low and non-existent sales on Etsy.

Stage 2 Self Shop Audit: Do You Need to Market More?

Okay, so you have a great product, beautiful images, well-written titles and descriptions, a cohesive and well-organized shop, and you're using all 13 tags, and you're still not seeing the sales roll in. It's probably time to take a look at your Etsy SEO (search engine optimization).

Take a look at your Etsy stats (right inside your Etsy dashboard). Are your listings being found and displayed by Etsy's search algorithm? For which keywords and phrases are they being found? Do these actually describe your item? If your listings aren't getting any views or are showing up for the wrong keywords, you may want to consider getting a monthly subscription with either eRank or Marmalead. These sites will help you identify keywords and phrases that both describe your product and get lots of queries from customers on Etsy. Even a month with one of these services can improve your sales drastically. If this sounds like an area you need to work on, check out Chapter 2 in the subsection about Titles for a lot more info on Etsy SEO.

If you've beefed up your Etsy SEO, have your listings and shop in order, and are still not getting the sales you want, it probably means you're just not getting enough eyeballs on your product. It might be time to invest some serious time, energy, and (perhaps) money into marketing and ads. There are also a few tricks you can employ to increase the number of eyes on your products, but none of these can make up for a half-baked or nonexistent marketing campaign. If you're interested in learning how to market your Etsy shop effectively, that's the focus of Book 2!

You might be thinking, isn't marketing for big corporations with loads of cash? Not at all. And like I said, we're going to cover ALL the good stuff about ads and marketing opportunities very shortly. But for now, here's your first step: Join a few relevant Etsy Teams (Google that—it's pretty easy to find). Etsy Teams allow you to collaborate with and learn from other similar sellers on Etsy. These sellers can share tips and tricks about how to sell your specific product on Etsy as well as the best channels for marketing that they've found to increase sales. Once you've found the marketing channels that work best for sellers like you, try them out—there are a number of free advertising channels available like social platforms and email marketing. Etsy also allows you to advertise within their platform and create sales and coupon codes to entice buyers. Try things one at a time, do what you can with the time and money you have, and watch your sales tick up. You've got this. Really. And again, if you'd like some instruction from yours truly on marketing efforts, just snag Book 2!

Duplicate Listing Trick

If you want a quick way to increase your listing impressions (views), you can list a single product multiple times using different keywords. This helps your listings appear for several different search results. This obviously only works if you plan to sell more than one of that particular item (I don't recommend you duplicate a listing for an original piece of art unless you're going to watch all those listings like a hawk to ensure you don't sell two at once). But, assuming you have many of the same product or create products on demand, you can copy the listings for that item and use a new title and new keywords (or simply a rearranged title and different variations of your original keywords) to target different search terms and potentially different customers.

This trick is best used by new sellers since it can help you figure out which keywords perform best for different products. And it can give you some initial sales if you've been in a slump. Because duplicating at least a few listings sends a lot of positive signals to Etsy's algorithm that can help a new shop get off the ground. However, be careful using this trick long term, when you're established as a seller. In fact, as your shop starts to grow I would avoid the practice entirely.

For one thing, if your shop is made up of a bunch of listings that are all virtually the same, anyone who actually visits your shop (instead of purchasing your listing straight from Etsy's search results page) is going to be pretty unimpressed by dozens of duplicated listings within each of your shop sections. And more and more these days, people click into Etsy shops to see what else the seller sells. You don't want to shoot your store in the foot by focusing too much on your individual listing's search result ranking.

A second downside to the duplicate listing trick is that there's a very real possibility that customers may see two of your identical listings side-by-side in the search results. Again, this looks tacky and can be confusing for buyers. This wasn't always the case. Etsy used to limit results from an individual shop to a single listing per results page. This is why older Etsy coaches often encourage the practice of duplicating listings as pretty much foolproof. But, nowadays, you need to be a little more careful.

Re-Listing Items

Again, if you're a new seller having trouble getting your listings to show up in search results, re-listing your items regularly can give you a slight edge. Re-listing is the practice of renewing a listing before it has expired (and paying another listing fee). This works because Etsy's search algorithm gives a nontrivial rank boost to new listings for the first few hours after they're listed.

If you think your listing is sending negative signals to Etsy's algorithms (e.g., you chose poor keywords to start out with), you can also do the following: duplicate your listing, then delete the original and start fresh with the new listing. That way, if your listing has inadvertently been sending negative signals to Etsy's algorithm that decrease its rank (e.g., if it's got a low conversion rate—which is pretty common for new listings in new shops), starting the item afresh with a new listing wipes out any "points" it has against it and gives it a new shot at ranking higher in search.

Ideally, you won't want to be re-listing items regularly forever. It can get expensive at $0.20 each time, and re-listing too often also prevents Etsy's algorithm from identifying what your item is and who best to display it to. As a new Etsy seller, you may feel that you would do a much better job than the algorithm at connecting your product with customers who want to buy it. After all, you know your product and your customers and Etsy clearly doesn't, at least at the beginning. But, part of selling through Etsy is trusting that the search algorithm will eventually figure it out and do a better job connecting you to customers than you could. And I promise it will—the algorithm can change much easier than our human minds can. It "learns" about your product over the life of a listing from an increasingly complicated web of signals that no person alone could navigate. And if you let Etsy's algorithm do its thing, you'll eventually find that it's connecting your product to customers you never would have found on your own (like people across the world!).

So, go ahead and use the re-listing trick, but be careful of overusing it. Etsy search is getting better and better, and your shop will succeed in the long-run not by tricking the algorithm, but by using it to its full potential.

Help! My Sales Just Dropped!

It's so frustrating to see some success in your Etsy shop, sure you're doing everything right, and then watch your sales suddenly plummet. If this happens, don't panic. It's normal for sales to go up and down week to week and season to season.

Here's some of the reasons you might see a drop (and what you can do about it).

Trends

One reason for dips in sales is "trends." Etsy's obsession with "trends" or "seasonality" means that its algorithm boosts listings based on when it believes the item will be most popular. Even for items that aren't seasonal, Etsy attaches a "season" (a number of weeks or months) to each listing, and when that season ends, the algorithm will suppress the listing in order to boost other products. The "season" can be a holiday like "Christmas," an event like "Wedding," or it can simply be the time period during which the item sold well the previous year. For example, certain rings and jewelry often get a boost in the late spring/early summer during what Etsy considers to be "wedding season." If you're interested in finding out what season your product most likely falls into, you can check out Etsy's yearly Trend Report (Google Etsy's Trend Report for the current year).

Etsy has Changed Something

Another reason for a drop in sales is that Etsy has updated their platform, which it does A LOT. Recently, Etsy changed the way sellers could advertise within Etsy, and the vast majority of sellers (I hesitate to say *all*, though I suspect it was all sellers) saw a drastic drop in how much money they were making through Etsy Ads (formerly Etsy Promoted Listings).

Etsy is also constantly updating its search algorithm to make the AI better. It's worth spending some time on the Etsy Forums and Etsy's blog watching for updates like these. For example, early in 2020, Etsy updated its search to recognize most pluralizations and many common misspellings. This meant that we could get rid of the "T-shirts" tag since we already had "T-shirt" and use that tag for another relevant keyword. Small changes like this may not impact your listings much in the moment, but if you miss a number of them in a row, you may find that your views and sales are dropping because your tags or titles are outdated.

It's wise to check regularly for algorithm changes. Someday, Etsy's algorithm might start looking at your descriptions for relevant keywords. Or it may stop rewarding keyword stuffing in titles. These would be BIG reforms that would rearrange the entire landscape of search results overnight. Etsy isn't doing this to make your life difficult. In fact, algorithm changes are supposed to make selling on

Etsy easier for both sellers and buyers. The trick is to stay on top of the reforms and change with the times.

You're Not Engaging with Your Shop Often Enough

When your Etsy shop is doing well, you might be tempted to ignore it and let it chug along, bringing in sales for the products you already have listed. The problem is that Etsy's algorithm rewards shops with sellers who are highly engaged, and when it notices that it's been weeks since you added a new listing, made a change to your shop, or improved an old listing, it will punish your listings by not displaying them as often or as high up in search results.

This reality is extremely irritating, especially since Etsy is considered a platform for hobby crafters and creators who don't necessarily want their shop to be an everyday, full-time job. The trick, though, is that you don't need to make major changes everyday to look like an engaged seller to Etsy's algorithm. You simply need to change *something* every few days or so. This can be as simple as updating your shop announcement once a week and swapping out a few keywords on a listing twice during the same week. If you've created a bunch of new products, stagger your listing uploads—add one Monday and the next one on Wednesday, then Friday—instead of putting them all up at once.

The more often you make even a small change to your Etsy shop, the more positive signals get sent to Etsy about your shop, which means each listing will rank better in search results. And the better your products are ranking, the more people will see them and buy them.

Help! My Account Was Suspended or Limited

Unfortunately, Etsy account suspensions do happen. Etsy has a reputation to uphold, and it protects its marketplace by closing or limiting shops that are breaking the rules or treating customers poorly. You can read about the differences between limited and suspended accounts and reasons this can happen in Etsy's help section "My Account has Been Suspended."

Odds are, however, sellers whose shops get limited or suspended have known there was a problem for a while. A member of Etsy's Trust and Safety Team will have emailed them alerting them to the problem (or usually pattern of problems) and tried to work with them to correct it. Contrary to the internet rumors, Etsy doesn't use automation to actually suspend accounts—their automation helps them recognize red flags, but an actual human reviews the flags and decides what course to pursue (you can read Etsy's official statement on Etsy's site.)

The most common reasons for account suspension are policy violations (a seller is selling stuff prohibited by Etsy) and truly terrible customer service (not fulfilling orders on time or at all; sending low-quality, broken or the wrong items to customers; discriminating against or disparaging customers, that kind of thing).

Make sure you've read "Etsy's House Rules" for sellers. And make sure your shipping timeframes are accurate. You'd be surprised at how often shops become "at risk for suspension" because their shipping times are too short and their orders get flagged by Etsy as "overdue" one too many times. Etsy also has options for sellers going through periods of hardship and can't continue filling orders for some reason. Sellers always have the option to pause their shop by placing it in "Vacation Mode." I'll talk more about this below, but vacation mode often means that a seller will have to start all over building up their shop when they unpause, even if the vacation was only for a week or two. But using vacation mode when you're struggling is way better than not fulfilling orders and risking Etsy closing your shop entirely.

If, after everything, you do find yourself in a situation where your account has been suspended, you can appeal. Etsy generally treats its sellers quite well and will give most sellers a second chance if they show they can fix the problem and abide by Etsy's rules.

Potential Pitfall: Shop Vacation Mode

One question that more Etsy shop owners SHOULD be asking (but often don't, they just do it) is whether they should be using "vacation mode" for their shop. Most sellers think "Oh, yep. I need a break. Vacation mode, activate!" without much thought for the consequences.

So here's the skinny:

Vacation Mode seems like such a wonderful option for those of us who are burned out and need a break from our shops, but unfortunately, vacation mode seems to send negative signals to Etsy's algorithm. The vast majority of sellers who pause their shops see sharp drops in sales and often feel like they're starting over trying to get their products recognized by Etsy search.

I mention this not necessarily to deter you from ever taking a vacation. Please, take time off when you need it! No one wants to be tied to their Etsy shop 24/7, 365 days a year. But if you do decide to take an extended leave of absence from your shop, know that it may take some time to work back up to the sales you were getting before the pause.

One option I've used (successfully) to both take a vacation and keep my shop open is to temporarily lengthen my shipping times. Instead of 6-10 business days, I changed my shipping temporarily to 2-3 weeks. I explained the change in my shop announcement (and told my customers that I was going to Thailand for two weeks so they'd understand) and put a large note at the top of each listing description about the slower shipping times. It meant that I could go enjoy my vacation and come back to plenty of orders without needing to put my shop on pause.

Help! I Need More Variations Options

So far, this chapter has been kind of heavy. I've given you the low-down about the scary problems you might run into as an Etsy seller like copyright infringement and account suspension. But sometimes, you just need advice on how to work around the limits of Etsy's seller platform. And one of the most common questions I see in this category is how to navigate variations when you need more than the two Etsy gives you.

Combine two options into one custom variation

Say you're selling helix earring studs. You offer three colors—gold, silver, and rose gold—and two different closure options—ball and labret—as well as four options for bar length—4mm, 6mm, 8mm, and 10mm. Since the *front* of the earring is the same, it makes a lot of sense to have one listing with all three variations as options for customers. But, of course, Etsy only allows you two.

What you can do in this case is offer a "Color" variation and combine the other two options into one custom variation called "Bar style + Length." You'd list the options in the second variation as "Ball end 4mm, Ball end 6mm, Ball end 8mm, Ball end 10mm, Labret 4mm, Labret 6mm...." You get the idea.

This also works for matching sets where you want to offer color and size options for each item in the set—mother/daughter tees, his and hers rings, that kind of thing.

Check a Box to Offer Different Prices or Quantities for Your Options

Say you sell glicée posters and want to list each size at a different price. In this case, you'll only need one variation, "Size," with the box next to "prices vary with each size" checked. Once you save and exit the variations pop-up, Etsy will allow you to fill in a custom price for each option. This is true for quantity as well. Say, you've made six pink baby blankets but only five blue. Check the box that says, "quantities vary," and Etsy will give you the option to set quantities for each option in your variation.

You can take these boxes even further if you need to also. For example, say you sell posters and want to offer different sizes and different finishes (gloss, matte, etc.) at different prices. If you click "prices vary" for BOTH of your variations, "Size" and "Finish," you'll be able to set different prices for each combination of variations—in other words, you'd be able to offer your "8x10 in gloss" option for $15 and your "8x10 in matte" for $17 and so on for the other size/finish option combos.

I won't give a million more examples because I think you get the idea. Play around with your variations and those "price" and "quantity" checkboxes until you find the ideal options for whatever you sell.

Use the Personalization Box

If you find that you need one more variation or your variation needs a bit more explanation than just "size" or "color," you can use the *personalization box.* Technically, this box was created for monogrammed items and custom orders and stuff like that, but you can use it creatively—for example, to simplify variations that have become unwieldy. I've used it when selling face masks—in addition to choosing "size" and "color" options, my customers could "personalize" their masks by letting me know if they wanted ribbon or elastic and if they wanted nose wire or not.

TIP: Make sure you keep variations the same across all similar listings, especially as your shop grows. It can get really hard to buy materials for a lot of orders if your options aren't consistent. I learned this the hard way. When I was ordering supplies for 10 on-demand orders a week, it was pretty easy to remember that "charcoal" and "dark gray" were the same color shirt, but as I scaled up, the discrepancies made ordering a nightmare. So, either use Etsy's standard variation options or, if you create your own, keep them consistent as you create additional listings.

Using Etsy's variations creatively allows you to sell lots of product through a single listing. It makes your store cleaner and easier to navigate, and it saves you money! Every four months, when Etsy automatically renews your listing whether it's selling or not, that's \$.20 saved for each variation you might have listed separately had you not known how to use variations.

99 Problems But Etsy Ain't One of Them

The good news is that most of the time, Etsy works really well. Bugs are usually manageable, and the more Etsy grows, the bigger its capacity will be for addressing issues quickly. Don't forget you have a whole army of other Etsy sellers on your side, who are going through the same things you are and thinking of creative solutions. So don't despair if you run into a roadblock. There's a solution to be found.

When it comes to troubleshooting as an Etsy seller, creative solutions are key. Instead of becoming daunted by the problems that arise, try to see them as an opportunity for growth. You got this.

READY TO GROW?
CHECK OUT BOOK 2

If you've applied the concepts in Book 1 and are working, step by step, to lay the foundation of your Etsy shop, take a moment to pat yourself on the back. The work you're doing will pave the way to steady success and reliable sales.

And the coolest part? You are now officially NOT a beginner Etsy seller. You've mastered that level. If that's all you need, I salute you. For some people, Etsy was never meant to be a full-scale effort. A side hobby is a fantastic option.

That said, if you are interested in ramping up growth and learning Etsy-specific strategies, this is your cue to move along to Book 2 of this series: *Marketing and Advertising Strategies for Etsy*.

It's an instruction manual on how to take your foundation and grow your shop into something bigger. We'll show you how to make your products more visible within Etsy and across the web, for higher sales volume and faster growth.

Made in the USA
Monee, IL
14 November 2024

70131942R00075